Personal Roots of Representation

Personal Roots of Representation

Barry C. Burden

PRINCETON UNIVERSITY PRESS
PRINCETON AND OXFORD

Published by Princeton University Press, 41 William Street, Princeton, New Jersey 08540
In the United Kingdom: Princeton University Press, 3 Market Place, Woodstock, Oxfordshire OX20 1SY

Library of Congress Cataloging-in-Publication Data
Burden, Barry C., 1971–
Personal roots of representation / Barry C. Burden.
p. cm.
Includes bibliographical references.
ISBN 978-0-691-12744-6 (hardcover : alk. paper)
ISBN 978-0-691-13459-8 (paper : alk. paper)
1. United States. Congress. 2. Legislators—United States—Attitudes.
3. Representative government and representation—United States. I. Title.
JK1021.B85 2007
328.73--dc22 2006102733

British Library Cataloging-in-Publication Data is available

This book has been composed in Sabon

Printed on acid-free paper. ∞

pup.princeton.edu

Printed in the United States of America

10 9 8 7 6 5 4 3 2 1

Contents

List of Figures and Tables

Figures

Tables

Acknowledgments

There are always many people to thank along the path from formative ideas to a rather different finished project. Pieces of the project benefited from presentation at the 2000 and 2004 American Political Science Association meetings, Harvard Political Psychology and Behavior Workshop, and Harvard American Politics Research Workshop. For comments on papers and chapters I thank Chris Adolph, Lauren Cohen Bell, Ben Bishin, David Campbell, John Gerring, John Hibbing, Sunshine Hillygus, William Howell, Patricia Hurley, Phil Jones, Andy Karch, Jane Mansbridge, Eric Schickler, Wendy Schiller, Donley Studlar, and Sidney Verba. Data were provided by Cliff Davidson, Bill Godshall, Keith Poole, Nina Shokraii Rees, Andrew Taylor, the Interuniversity Consortium for Political and Social Research (ICPSR), the Thomas web site http://thomas.loc.gov, and the Policy Agendas Project courtesy of Frank Baumgartner and Bryan Jones. None of these individuals or institutions is responsible for the use or interpretation of data here. Financial support was provided by the Clark/Cooke fund at Harvard, and research support was provided by Phil Jones, who read every word of the draft manuscript. I appreciate the time set aside by the former members of Congress I interviewed and to the Kennedy School of Government for making them available to the academic community. I also appreciate a certain chain of coffee shops for providing comfortable seats and hot java to encourage my writing. Laura, Davis, and Samantha were by far the most accommodating of my work and deserve all my gratitude.

Personal Roots of Representation

CHAPTER ONE

Personal Roots of Representation

RICK SANTORUM AND ARLEN SPECTER were something of an odd couple when it comes to Washington politics. Although both were United States senators representing Pennsylvania, and both are Republican, their policy views could not have been more divergent. One sought compromise and generally avoided hot-button issues; the other was defined by such issues. Santorum was chair of the Republican conference in the Senate and an advocate of conservative policies, particularly on sensitive social issues such as abortion and gay marriage. Specter is pro-choice and often bucks his party, to the point of generating backlash from Republican colleagues. These fundamental differences in their preferences affected not only their voting records but their decisions about which issues to tackle.

Particularly on domestic social issues, it is difficult to overstate the differences that separate the two senators. As *Congressional Quarterly* put it, "An unalloyed social conservative, Santorum saves his toughest fights for the issue of abortion. He is a leader in the fight to outlaw a procedure that opponents call 'partial birth' abortion, which he has called 'barbaric' and 'the calculated killing of the nearly born.'"[1] Specter, in contrast, is one of the few true moderates left in Congress. Some of his Republican colleagues in the Senate even challenged his position as chair of the Judiciary Committee when he suggested that conservative judicial nominees would get serious scrutiny. *CQ* reports that, unlike Santorum, "Specter fights to soften anti-abortion language in the GOP platform, tries to outdo Democrats on education spending, and not infrequently votes with Democrats on issues such as extending unemployment benefits and allowing patients to sue their managed-care health plans." Although a four-term senator, he barely managed to win the 2004 Republican primary election in which he faced a more conservative challenger.

As one summary indicator of their differences, consider Poole and Rosenthal's measure of legislative ideology known as NOMINATE. Their procedure uses roll call votes to place legislators on a unidimensional scale where -1 is most liberal and $+1$ is most conservative. By this yardstick,

[1] This and other *Congressional Quarterly* (*CQ*) quotations in this chapter come from *CQ's Politics in America 2004: The 108th Congress*, ed. David Hawkings and Brian Nutting. Washington, DC: CQ Press. Retrieved from CQ Electronic Library, CQ Congress Collection. <http://library.cqpress.com/congress/>.

Santorum came in at .44, making him the 15th most conservative senator in the 108th Congress. Specter was located at .06, ranking him 51st in a chamber of 100. Nearly every other roll call indicator shows the same gulf between the two, a gap that is larger than that between the political parties themselves.

Why were Santorum and Specter so different, not only in their positions but in their policy priorities? Unfortunately, the usual suspects that congressional scholars line up to explain policy differences do not provide much of an answer. Were they from different states, a constituency focus would be the place to start. But they shared a common constituency in Pennsylvania, so electoral explanations cannot be responsible for the differences. Pennsylvania politics tend to be bifurcated between the eastern and western ends of the state, so it is possible that Santorum and Specter divide up the state geographically.[2] Yet the differences in their voting records are far greater than demographic differences between Pittsburgh and Philadelphia would dictate. Both Santorum and Specter were seasoned politicians with years of congressional experience (and law degrees), thus rendering career-based explanations unhelpful. Finally, and most obviously, both senators were Republicans, rendering a partisan explanation for their actions moot. If career, constituency, and party affiliation fail, what accounts for the stark differences between Santorum and Specter? In reviewing their cases, the importance of more personal factors becomes obvious.

As a start, consider some facts about Santorum's background. His *CQ* biography documents, "The son of an Italian immigrant—a Veterans Administration psychologist—the boyish-faced Santorum stresses individual responsibility and self-reliance, not government assistance programs. He can draw on his own experience of holding down a full-time job while attending law school." Knowing just this, it might not be especially surprising that Santorum is conservative on fiscal matters.

But Santorum is best known for his activism on social issues, primarily his opposition to abortion, gay marriage, and stem cell research. He is a devout Catholic who attends Mass daily[3] and held a course on Catholicism for fellow Republican members of Congress.[4] He even helped convert fellow senator Sam Brownback (R-KS) to Catholicism. A former aide

[2] Schiller (2000) shows that even same-party senators from the same state can form differing electoral coalitions. Fiorina (1974), Huntington (1950), and Shapiro et al. (1990) all offer some version of the "two constituencies" thesis, although they stress states where senators represent different parties.

[3] Claud R. Marx, "Religious and Personal Issue Drive Santorum on Abortion," Associated Press, 20 October 1999.

[4] Mark Leibovich, "Father First, Senator Second," *Washington Post,* 18 April 2005, p. C1.

went so far as to call him "a Catholic missionary who happens to be in the Senate."[5]

Despite the obvious importance of Santorum's faith, he did not immediately tackle difficult morality issues when first elected to Congress. He was conservative on social matters but not especially active. "Santorum was pro-life from the time he first ran for Congress, but it wasn't an issue he was vocal about. Santorum never gave a speech about abortion in the House or Senate until the late-term-abortion debates of 1996 and 1997."[6] The timing of this shift from passive to active opposition corresponds to a critical event in Santorum's personal life.

In 1996 Santorum's wife, Karen, was due with their fourth child. The pregnancy suffered from complications, and doctors warned that the baby had a fatal defect. Twice the doctors proposed aborting the fetus, an idea that the Santorums rejected. To cope with the pregnancy's uncertainty, Karen began writing letters to the unborn child, already named Gabriel Michael Santorum. As doctors warned, Gabriel was born prematurely at five months and lived only a couple of hours outside the womb. Rather than follow standard protocol, the Santorums took the body home rather than to a funeral home and changed a hospital form's description from "20-week-old fetus" to "20-week-old baby."[7] Although understandably upset about the outcome, Santorum was nonetheless satisfied that Gabriel died "naturally" rather than by an abortive "murder." Now the father of six children, Santorum holds memories of Gabriel close. He keeps a framed photo of the baby on his desk. His wife's prenatal letters to Gabriel were published as a book that condemns "infanticide" and "partial-birth abortion" while advocating for her husband's renewed fight against such practices in the Senate. Santorum believes that Gabriel's death intensified his views about abortion, which he now sees as the great moral issue facing America. His intensity about the issue clearly stems from personal experience.

Arlen Specter's values come from an entirely different orientation, but likewise have their roots in life experience. They start not with religion but with a prosecutorial nose for the facts. A former district attorney, Specter is known for his tenaciousness, strong work ethic, and especially his independence (Fenno 1991). His independent streak motivated him to switch parties early in his career to increase his chances of winning office. Specter is also the son of a Russian immigrant and one of just a few Jewish Republicans in Congress. When called "ambitious," Specter "reaches

[5] Michael Sokolove, "The Believer," *New York Times Magazine*, 22 May 2005, p. 58.

[6] Leibovich, "Father First, Senator Second."

[7] Leibovich, "Father First, Senator Second."

back to his immigrant roots," saying, "When I was a growing up ambition was not only a good word in our household, it was an indispensable word" (quoted in Fenno 1991, 5).

Specter was never a typical Republican on social issues, and became less so over time as the party moved rightward in the 1980s and 1990s. Being largely pro-choice in a strongly pro-life party is challenging, as is representing the many Catholic and other antiabortion voters in Pennsylvania. Immediately after his first Senate victory Specter realized, "My toughest issue is abortion." But he maintained his moderate position because, he said, "I'm convinced I'm on the right side" (quoted in Fenno 1991, 28). Yet abortion is not a great moral imperative for Specter, and he generally avoids making much commotion around the issue. His floor votes on abortion-related matters are generally centrist, and speeches on the issue are nonexistent.

The same cannot be said for health care, where he is an activist driven by deep personal experience. It began in 1993 when Specter complained to doctors that he suffered from pain in his face and neck. He suspected a brain tumor was responsible and asked for an MRI (magnetic resonance imaging) scan. His doctors declined the request because he showed no signs of memory loss or other common symptoms. Only after demanding it was Specter given the MRI; the test that revealed a two-inch brain tumor.[8] Fortunately, the tumor was benign and could be removed with surgery, but the experience had an indelible impact.

Specter returned to the Senate soon after the surgery with a new scar on his head and a new attitude toward national health care policy. He immediately became an advocate of access to medical screening technology and preventive medicine. As chair of the Appropriations subcommittee dealing with health, he held some of the first hearings on breast cancer screenings. Specter argued that mammograms ought to be available to all women under 40, noting his own experience, in which a brain scan helped find a life-threatening tumor.[9] Close observers of the budget process believe that the National Institutes of Health (NIH) get more funding than they would without Specter's support.[10]

In sharp contrast to Santorum, Specter was also an early proponent of embryonic stem cell research. He became an even stronger advocate about the time he was diagnosed with Hodgkin's lymphoma, a cancerous condition that was treated with chemotherapy. Upon introducing another

[8] Sharon Voas, "What Limits to Health Care?" *Pittsburgh Post-Gazette,* 21 July 1993, p. A1.

[9] Judy Packer-Tursman, "Senators Back Early Mammograms," *Pittsburgh Post-Gazette,* 6 February 1996, p. A10.

[10] Bill Swindell, "Labor-HHS-Education Conferees Wrangle over Size of NIH Increase," *CQ Weekly,* 18 October 2003, p. 2562.

bill to support therapeutic cloning in early 2005, Specter explained that his condition might have been treated with stem cell therapies if they had been supported by federal policies. Referring to his obvious hair loss caused by chemotherapy, Specter stated, "I've got a new hairdo, which you can all observe, and that is indicative of a problem which may well be helped by stem cell research if it were to go forward."[11] While several other senators joined his effort, Specter attracted attention and credibility because of his firsthand experience. "I don't choose to unduly personalize it, but I have to find some way to excuse my hairdo." Aside from Orrin Hatch (R-UT), who also had personal reasons for supporting such research, few Republicans were willing to buck President Bush and their party on the issue.

The lesson to be taken from Santorum and Specter is the potential for representatives' experiences, interests, and expertise to shape their actions, what I call the personal roots of representation. Although the usual suspects of partisanship and constituency preferences surely play a role in guiding representatives' actions in general, those two factors are far from determinative, even on some of the most salient issues in contemporary American politics. Santorum's and Specter's legislative preferences on specific issues are more complex than the current political science formulation allows. More importantly, their differences are not limited to positions taken in roll call votes. They also choose to be active on different sets of issues, with Santorum pushing for limits on abortion and Specter supporting access to health care and aggressive stem cell research.

This book is about the preferences that drive all of the Rick Santorums and Arlen Specters who inhabit the modern Congress. Their cases demonstrate that legislative preferences cannot be boiled down to partisanship and constituent interests. Preferences depend on a wider range of phenomena, including the backgrounds of legislators themselves. The information gleaned, and the interests and values formed, from life experiences shape their behavior on roll call votes, and more importantly and frequently, their proactive leadership on a smaller set of issues.

Unpacking Legislative Preferences

What members of Congress do surely depends on what their constituents want. Representatives are generally in tune with their constituents when it comes to broad orientations toward public policy. As I elaborate in chapter 2, evidence shows that liberal districts tend to elect liberal legis-

[11] Kevin Freking, "Ailing Specter Now Pushes Stem Cell Research." *Washington Post*, 21 April 2005.

lators, and conservative districts typically have conservative representatives. The bird's-eye view strongly suggests that constituents are mostly getting what they want, just as the "delegate" view of representation expects. Yet I contend that this highly aggregated approach to assessing representation misses important deviations from public opinion. Relying only on summary information culled from many districts and many issues often leads to the false conclusion that legislators are strictly controlled by their constituents. But legislators can deviate from their constituents' preferences. Why might they be allowed to do so?

Elections are thought to be the main mechanism by which legislators are held accountable. Madison argued as much in the Federalist Papers, and scholarly wisdom has long held that an unrepresentative legislator will be defeated by one whose policies are closer to the voters. Building on the median voter theorem, Downs (1957) made that point about party politicians, and Mayhew (1974) applied the logic of pandering to members of the House. The fear of losing one's seat ought to be enough for the representative to act on constituents' desires.

While the power of elections to motivate politicians is quite real, there are two main reasons why they are not sufficient to guarantee full policy representation. First, voters are only permitted to choose candidates, not policies. A candidate represents a bundle of policies, many of which are inconsistent, not well formed, or unknown to voters (McCrone and Kuklinski 1979). With only two candidates to choose from in most elections, voters will not find a candidate with whom they agree on every issue. Many congressional elections instead revolve around a small number of highly salient issues at the expense of many other matters that are likely to be on the legislative agenda. The ballot is just too crude an instrument to send finely tuned messages on desired policies.

Second, most subpresidential elections in the United States are not seriously contested. Only a few dozen of the 435 House races held every two years are truly competitive in the sense that both candidates have a reasonable chance of winning (Jacobson 2004). About three out of every 20 House elections are not contested at all (Wrighton and Squire 1997). The spatial voting model, in which voters choose candidates nearest their positions, only applies when candidates are equally credible and equally able to communicate with voters. When candidates have advantages in name recognition, staffing, and funding, they can deviate from public opinion to some degree without jeopardizing their seats (Burden 2004a). Indeed, members of Congress intentionally cultivate their constituencies to generate trust and leeway in policy (Bianco 1994; Fenno 1978). Public opinion would have more substantial influence on governing behavior if legislators feared retribution for not heeding it, but warding off competition dampens the influence of constituents. Because elections are inadequate to ensure that voters' views on policy are fully represented by candidates, legislators will never perfectly represent the policy wishes of their constituents.

In a principal-agent framework used in economics, the job of the constituent is to monitor what legislators do. As the principal, the median voter in the district employs an agent in Washington to act on her behalf. I have already argued that the principal faces a difficult task because neither fear of replacement nor strict monitoring will be sufficient to ensure the agent's compliance. In this framework we should thus expect slack between constituents' preferences and legislators' actions, or what is known in much of the literature as "shirking."[12] When constituents' views are not represented, it is usually assumed that the legislator is "shirking" his duties to pursue his own self-interest (Bender and Lott 1996; Uslaner 2002). But this reasoning jumps too quickly to a conclusion about the causes of slack. While identifying the *degree* of disagreement is a useful indicator of how much leeway a legislator has, the shirking approach says little about the *causes* of such slack. As I explain in chapter 2, it is not enough to estimate how much shirking there is; it is imperative to understand why it exists in the first place.

Portraying the situation as a contest between constituents' preferences and the legislator's ideology alone assumes a false dichotomy. Many factors shape legislative behavior. Among them are pressure from interest groups, party influence, cues from the administration, media priming, and logrolling among members. As a result, the standard "delegate" versus "trustee" paradigm that is so heavily used in legislative studies oversimplifies the task of understanding how representatives behave. The delegate model may be a useful standard of evaluation, since such a legislator simply follows her constituents' wishes (assuming they can be identified). But if the trustee model is the only alternative to full policy representation, deciding which is correct unnecessarily distracts researchers from asking important questions about other influences.

To evaluate the health of republican government, it is critical for one to know the conditions under which a legislator heeds or dismisses the opinions of his constituency. Researchers must begin decomposing policy shirking into its constituent elements. To offer a medical analogy, a doctor cannot evaluate a person's health knowing only how much cholesterol is in his blood. The type of cholesterol is just as important. In addition to other indicators, the physician needs to distinguish between high-density lipoproteins and low-density lipoproteins (HDL and LDL), otherwise known as "good" and "bad" cholesterol. Although bad cholesterol can

[12] Shirking is also used to explain why less effort may be exerted by legislators in their final terms (Bender and Lott 1996). I focus solely on policy shirking.

clog artery walls, good cholesterol actually helps clear blood vessels. Likewise, the total amount of shirking or policy leeway is only properly understood when the reasons for it are known. The total amount of shirking is a function of both "good" and "bad" variables. In the final chapter of the book I will suggest which forms of shirking might be considered desirable and which undesirable.

This approach points the study of congressional representation in a new direction. I care not only *where* a politician stands in relation to her constituents, but *why* and with *what consequences*. Abstract ideological preferences can be measured reasonably well, but we must unpack them to understand how the member came to his positions and how they motivate legislative action. Two legislators might take positions contrary to their constituencies for different reasons. The first could do so for principled reasons. She might have chosen her position by reasoning from a broader philosophy of government or because of expertise that most constituents lack. The second legislator might have less noble motives. His party leaders pressured him to take the position, or an interest group's lobbying was effective. Both members have shirked, but for quite different reasons.

Levels of legislative shirking are important too, perhaps more important in the early stages of the lawmaking process than the eventual positions themselves. On many issues, legislators merely vote on the relevant roll calls as the come, but on a small set of issues a legislator becomes much more heavily involved. Time is a precious resource, and most of a legislator's time is spent on just a handful of issues. As players in particular domains of policy, they give speeches, influence colleagues, and sponsor legislation. If these issues happen to be the ones on which they differ from their constituents, the degree of deviation is more severe than it would be if only roll call votes were at stake. Proactive behavior by legislators upstream in the policy process largely determines the agenda that other legislators will vote on.

Innovations

My perspective encourages a different empirical approach than is usually taken in the study of Congress. The typical study tries to explain general roll call voting patterns, lumping all members into a single analysis. When an explanatory variable such as party affiliation turns out to be a statistically significant predictor, the researcher concludes that partisanship causes legislators' voting patterns. Although this can be a useful enterprise, I believe that it misses much of congressional reality.

There are three ways in which my approach diverges from this standard method. First, I examine activity on specific policies rather than general indicators of preferences or activity levels. The prototypic congressional study relies on NOMINATE scores (Poole and Rosenthal 1997) or ratings by interest groups as indicators of a legislator's ideology. Which of these general measures is used does not matter much (Burden, Caldeira, and Groseclose 2000) since each one implies a similar view of representation. Each roll call scoring technique assumes that the member's actions across a wide range of issues can be summarized by a single position. Roll call voting is often the only standard by which legislative activity is judged. Yet it would be a grave mistake to assume that every issue is defined on the left-right continuum just because such ideological scales can be constructed. This approach also assumes that legislative activities prior to the vote itself are inconsequential. In later chapters, I challenge both of these ideas. Exploding these assumptions makes an issue-by-issue approach more appropriate. Even after controlling for general ideological preferences and previous levels of support for a position, I am able to identify member-specific factors that drive legislators' positions and their attention to issues. The experiences of Rick Santorum and Arlen Specter show that these personal factors can have more influence on congressional behavior than is commonly thought.

Second, my theory encourages analysis of legislators in the majority and minority separately. I argue that the effects of many of the member-specific variables are asymmetric across parties, depending on whether the party is a proponent or opponent of the policy status quo. Generally speaking, threat motivates more personal involvement than does opportunity. The tendency to throw all legislators into a single analysis hides these important distinctions. I demonstrate this point in several cases by first analyzing all representatives simultaneously, then separating by party to show the differential effects of members' traits. I would reason, for example, that religious faith and personal health experiences affect Santorum and Specter much more than they would two equivalent Senate Democrats.

Third, and building on the first two points, I contrast proactive and reactive behavior. Proactive behavior is action that requires initiative. It includes doing research outside of committee, lobbying fellow members, contacting interest groups, making floor speeches, and introducing and cosponsoring legislation. Although the range of possible proactive behaviors is great, for tractability I focus on speechmaking and bill cosponsorship. What all proactivity has in common is that it requires a conscious decision by the legislator to take action in advance of a floor vote. As Hall (1993) has shown, members only have enough resources to be active on a handful of issues, and their decisions about which issues to take up are not made lightly. The factors that explain proactive behavior are quite consequential in the process of representation since proactive behavior magnifies a legislator's influence. Reactive behavior, in contrast, is a passive response to decisions made by others. The quintessential reactive behavior is roll call voting. Because research on Congress focuses so heavily on roll calls, we know little about the forces that differentiate the two kinds of actions (Van Doren 1990). If constituents or personal traits have different effects on reactive and proactive behavior, as I argue they do, then the distinction is critical empirically, theoretically, and normatively. Santorum's and Specter's backgrounds are responsible for their differing roll call records across a wide range of bills, but they play an even more substantial role in motivating proactivity on a small set of issues.

As a corollary to these three innovations, I ask whether campaign contributors are aware of how legislators' personal traits affect their behavior. In several cases I discover that patterns of giving by political action committees (PACs) are indeed sensitive to representatives' backgrounds. PACs give more money to those with experiences sympathetic to their interests, even after accounting for partisanship, constituency preferences, and other factors. Not only do legislators' personal roots shape their lawmaking activities, but they also affect how much campaign money can be raised, which in turn shapes their odds of reelection.

In addition to these three innovations, the book's strength comes from its multimethod approach. I develop a theory based on a variety of literatures in political science and economics, but it is also informed by in-depth qualitative interviews with several former members of Congress. The interviews help ground the study and inform the hypotheses to be tested. I also conduct extensive quantitative analysis of legislative behavior, both reactive and proactive. In three different policy domains, I examine the propositions listed above and find support for the theory.

Descriptively, I have argued that policy representation is not perfect, in that constituents do not get exactly the policies they would like. From a normative standpoint, it could even argued that constituents *should not* get everything they want. Voters are less informed and deliberate less than legislators, yet this does not mean that legislators are always right. One might argue that the collective views of several hundred thousand constituents in a House district might effectively counter any biases contained in a single representative (Page and Shapiro 1992).[13] The structure of Congress, with its committee-based system of expertise and moderately strong parties, does not always encourage policy responsiveness. The influence of party leaders, lobbyists, campaign activists, and the administration can pull members away from district concerns. These institutional factors have been studied at length. As important as these forces are, their

[13] On a related note, Weissberg (1978) suggests that collective representation is more successful than the dyadic form of representation I emphasize (cf. Hurley 1982).

effects are also inconsistent as one moves from issue to issue. New coalitions must be assembled on each piece of legislation. Party leaders are strong in one domain, but weak in another. Interest groups wield influence in one issue area but not others. More lasting are the traits of members themselves. Legislators acquire expertise, values, and interests long before they arrive in Washington. These early influences often lead to more intense preferences that have the potential to deter other influences, even pressure from constituents. The limits of policy representation are often found in the representative himself.

As I shall argue, voters would do better to elect someone who is like them than to hope to change a representative who is not. In the language of economics, a principal would be better served to find a like-minded agent who does not require monitoring than to attempt control a potentially disobedient agent. Elections are a more powerful mechanism for enhancing representation when constituents are able to choose a candidate who already shares their value systems. Although elected officials certainly monitor public opinion, it can be difficult for citizens to change legislators' behavior on all but the most symbolic of issues. To the degree that the principal-agent framework adequately describes the relationship between the district and the representative, it must be enforced by selection at the outset, not conversion thereafter (Bernstein 1989). As a result, much of the policy representation that happens in Washington can be thought of as coincidental, at least in the sense that the representative happens to act in a way that constituents condone, rather than being controlled by voters.

The Rest of the Book

The remainder of the book explores the personal roots of representation. In chapter 2 I begin unpacking the concept of legislative "preferences" so often used by congressional scholars. In reviewing this literature, it seems ironic that most studies of policy responsiveness look at ideological behavior rather than policy itself. I develop a theory of legislator preferences that identifies why representatives position themselves as they do on particular issues, and what consequences these positions have. I propose values, information, and self-interest as three mechanisms that allow personal characteristics to be influential. The theory thus goes beyond taking generic "preferences" as mere starting points in explaining congressional activity by decomposing the *sources* of these preferences.

The dominant view among academics is that preferences are induced by constituents' pressure. These preferences are mostly *reactive* and affect the tail end of the policy process—roll call votes—since they are best suited for taking a position. But this focus on roll call votes both overstates and understates the role of constituents in determining legislator behavior. Often a legislator will act in a way consistent with constituents' preferences without purposely representing the district. The prevalence of coincidental factors means that analysis of roll call votes alone, particularly without measures of legislators' interests, will overstate the degree of constituent control. Yet legislators can also enhance the influence of constituency wishes by being more active on a few issues of great concern to the people they represent.

I point to many cases where legislators, purposely and often actively, deviate from district opinion. In these situations their preferences are induced by other forces, some of which emanate from within the legislator herself. My interviews with six former legislators, coupled with a series of examples from the media, highlight the importance of appreciating the complexity of legislative preferences.

The next three chapters each apply the theory to a different policy area. The most comprehensive of the applications, chapter 3 analyzes policymaking around tobacco and smoking. I begin by describing the "tobacco wars" of the 1990s to establish the context in which defenders of tobacco were especially threatened by policy change on the way. I estimate regression models that explain why legislators take pro- or antitobacco control actions in the 104th House. In addition to standard controls such as legislators' ideological predispositions, partisanship, and district interests in the tobacco industry, I find that representatives' personal tobacco use exerts direct and independent effects on their behavior. As defenders of the status quo, members who smoke are more likely to vote against, speak in opposition to, and sponsor bills to limit tobacco control measures ranging from advertising and sales prohibitions to ending of tobacco farm subsidies. Efforts in favor of tobacco control, in contrast, appear largely unrelated to personal and district ties to the industry and are more entrepreneurial in nature. Moreover, tobacco PACs appear to have identified sympathetic members of Congress and provide them with significantly more contributions than are given to other members with similar partisan or ideological predispositions.

Chapter 4 examines recent education policymaking, specifically vouchers and other school choice plans. Proposed reforms in the 1990s offered school choice and threatened the educational status quo of public education. I analyze action on a voucher initiative and more general voting patterns on education policy in the 107th House. Although school choice efforts have a strong partisan basis—with Republicans more likely than Democrats to favor alternatives to public schools—members' actions are also products of their districts' educational needs and their own experiences with school systems. Members with school-age children are more like to be active on the issue. Perhaps more importantly, legislators whose children are in public school are less likely to vote for a school voucher program. In addition, the relationships for threatened Democrats appear more conditional on the confluence of district and personal interests, again pointing to the imbalance in participation rates between the two sides of the issue. Finally, I show that teacher union PACs were sensitive to the school choices made by representatives. Legislators who sent their children to public school were more likely to receive contributions, particularly so if they were Democrats.

Chapter 5 analyzes a class of new ethical issues that include stem cell research, tax incentives for religious charities, and legal protection of religious practices. In each of these three cases I demonstrate that legislators' religious faiths affected their behavior. The personal influences were greatest among Republicans who were most defensive of the status quo at the time and in early proactive stages of the lawmaking process, where participation is selective. In addition, I find that members of smaller religious denominations who faced greater threats were especially motivated to support the religious liberties protection bill.

The book concludes in chapter 6 by reviewing the theoretical argument and summarizing the findings across the three policy applications. I point to ways in which the conventional understanding of congressional policymaking has missed important relationships that govern the connections between legislators and their constituents. Elections are not especially efficient means for constituent influence over policy unless they result in the selection of like-minded representatives. While the electoral connection is often powerful on a select set of issues where constituents' concerns are most salient, the nature of congressional deliberation allows for a great deal of policy shirking, both reactive and proactive. I also evaluate the normative value of deviation from constituency preferences using my theory as a guide. Determining the conditions under which legislators disregard constituents' wishes provides a new perspective on policy representation in the United States, one that appreciates the fundamental motivations that cause elected officials to do what they do.

CHAPTER TWO

A Theory of Legislative Preferences

> "Who are we when we're elected to the Senate?," asked Senator Warren Rudman (R-NH) rhetorically. "We are men and women. We are not bland, neutral, blank-slate people who never suffered, and never were happy. You tend to be influenced by the sum total of life's experiences."[1]

As a member of Congress, Warren Rudman was aware of a basic truth that most political scientists have for too long ignored. Researchers tend to assume that legislators either work only on behalf of their constituents or as foot soldiers for their political parties. In both of these approaches the legislator is viewed as little more than an automaton acting on behalf of someone else. Seldom do congressional scholars acknowledge what experiences members of Congress bring to the table. As Rudman points out, these experiences are substantial. They help a representative distill information, guide a member's decision making, and motivate action, just as they do for everyday people. Although legislators must be responsive to their districts, party leaders, and other actors in the polity, I contend they also heed their own internal cues.

This focus naturally invokes Pitkin's (1967) distinction between "descriptive" and "substantive" representation. Briefly stated, descriptive representation emphasizes the representative's personal characteristics and the degree to which the legislature "looks like" the population it represents. The descriptive model's emphasis is on whether members mirror the electorate's characteristics adequately rather than what the members actually do in office. Substantive representation, in contrast, occurs when representatives act on behalf of constituents' interests. This is the classic "delegate" view of representation in which legislators take instruction from constituents about how to act on their behalf.

Pitkin defines descriptive and substantive representation as alternatives, and later research assumes them to be independent of one another (Eulau and Karps 1977).[2] Recent debates about racial redistricting typically posit

[1] Laura Blumenfeld, "When Politics Becomes Personal," *Washington Post,* 19 June 1996, P. C1

[2] Mansbridge (2003) outlines four other forms of representation beyond the dyadic policy focus applied here.

an adversarial relationship between the two. In highlighting the "sum total of life's experiences" to which Rudman refers, I am instead arguing for the direct substantive consequences of descriptive traits. Descriptive representation often results in substantive representation. Although descriptive representation might have effects beyond policymaking, I emphasize the impact that legislators' interests, values, and expertise have on their substantive activities.

This approach turns scholarly attention away from the literature's recent reliance on the nebulous concepts of "ideology" and "preferences" as the only explanations for congressional behavior. A focus on legislators' preferences is not wrong, but it is incomplete. The black box of preferences requires unpacking for both analytic and evaluative purposes. Without considering from where these preferences originate, research on congressional politics is unable to tell us why members do what they do and how one might judge these factors normatively.

Assessing the effects of their preferences requires more careful attention to who representatives are. While it is useful for many analytical purposes, treating legislators as points in ideological space is certainly not realistic. The personal traits of members of Congress—not just race and sex, but others that are more difficult to observe—shape decision making in Washington. The reason, just as Rudman contends, is that background characteristics often suggest the kinds of predispositions that members bring with them to Congress.

Existing research assumes that members are continually looking *outward* for cues about how to legislate. They attend to district interests, consult with other members, listen to party leaders, are lobbied by interest groups, and are pressured by the president. The representative, in this view, is always working for someone else. Without dismantling this architecture entirely, I wish also to highlight the internal cues that members take. Members routinely reflect on their own interests, expertise, and information in choosing what to do. Mansbridge points out that "legislators often vote by 'introspective representation'" (1999, 644).[3] By this, she means that legislators look back on their own experiences and policy ideas. In her account, introspective representation is particularly potent when an issue is not yet crystallized in the party system or is new to most legislators because policy cues from other actors are scarce. The issues I examine—tobacco regulation, school choice, and faith-based policy—are of precisely that type. I will have more to say about the generality of my results in the conclusion, but the evidence will show that on several of the major issues of the past two decades members frequently used

[3] Later this is subsumed under what Mansbridge (2003) calls "gyroscopic representation."

introspective representation in deciding how to vote and especially whether to be active on an issue.

Introspective influences probably do not trump partisanship and constituency opinion on most roll call votes. Yet I believe that the conditions under which personal characteristics matter are widespread and predictable. I theorize that introspection is more powerful once one shifts the analysis away from the ubiquitous roll call vote to more active, and thus selective, forms of policymaking. Even on well-formed issues, personal characteristics can be powerful determinants of legislative activity upstream in the policy process.

There are endless anecdotes floating around Washington that document where personal motivations encouraged public action. The most dramatic are those in which an intense experience lit a fire under a member to pursue a cause. These stories tend to make news because they are gripping, and because they sometimes pit a member against her party. But they are also discounted by scholars because they are idiosyncratic. While not downplaying the importance of the isolated event or socialization experience that shapes a member's outlook, the social scientist simply finds it difficult to document these effects in a systematic way.

Anecdotal Evidence

Situations frequently arise in which a member of Congress experienced a dramatic personal event and became an advocate of policy change. There is no shortage of evidence that members engage in introspective representation. Although these cases might be atypical, they make it into the media with remarkable regularity. Collectively the anecdotes suggest that something systematic is happening that academics have been reluctant to acknowledge. Consider the following examples culled from the recent news.

Stem cell research, a policy area I take up in more detail in chapter 5, has seen support—and opposition—from unexpected corners. In the wake of the Bush administration's restrictions on embryonic stem cell research in 2001, Representative Diana DeGette (D-CO) began a push for more federal funding. DeGette has a 10-year-old daughter with diabetes and has consequently taken the lead on the issue out of an obvious personal connection to the issue.[4] Even more surprising, Mormon Orrin Hatch (R-UT) became a lead sponsor of the bill in the Senate. He also authored a letter, signed by 58 senators, asking President Bush to relax restrictions on, and increase funding for, stem cell research. The disparate

[4] Diane Carman, "Group's Hope Stems from Research," *Denver Post*, 20 January 2005, p. B01.

group behind the effort ranges from antiabortion Mormons like Hatch, Catholic Ted Kennedy (D-MA), and moderate Arlen Specter (R-PA). All have specific, but quite personal reasons, for pursuing stem cell research. These personal motivations not only influence how they vote on the floor but the amount of time they devote to the issue.

Firsthand experience with health concerns often has strong and lasting effects on a legislator. Senator Pete Domenici (R-NM) became active on mental health issues after his daughter's mental health condition became known.

> If it were not for Clare's struggle with what was finally diagnosed as atypical schizophrenia, it is improbable that Pete Domenici . . . would have assumed the unlikely role of champion for the mentally ill. "I don't believe the subject ever would have come up," he acknowledged.[5]

Although Domenici's legislative preferences reflect his Senate committee assignments, New Mexico constituents, and obligations to the Republican caucus, his decisions about which issues to tackle have personal roots as well.

> It is strange to think that government works that way, that the fact that a senior senator has a mentally ill daughter can spur governmental action on mental issues. Yet on many issues, politics really is that personal and lawmaking that arbitrary.

As the stem cell bill illustrates, common experiences can create strange bedfellows. As one observer put it, Domenici's involvement in mental health "has the flavor of Nixon in China." In addition, liberals including Paul Wellstone (D-MN) and Lynn Rivers (D-MI) joined forces with conservatives Alan Simpson (R-WY) and Domenici to push for new mental health coverage. Each suffered personally or vicariously through a family member's depression or a related mental illness. "'There has been a personal, crystallizing experience in each of our lives,' Wellstone says. 'You almost wish it didn't have to work that way.'" It is widely understood on the Hill that the Americans with Disabilities Act (ADA) of 1990 was largely guided to passage by members with disabled family members. Representative Tony Coelho (D-CA), primary author of the ADA, had epilepsy, as did Steny Hoyer's (D-MD) wife. Among other shepherds of the bill, Congressman Lowell Weicker's (R-CT) son had Down's syndrome and Tom Harkin's (D-IA) brother was deaf (Shapiro 1993). So important are personal and family brushes with health concerns that the American Cancer Society has adopted a celebrity-based approach in its

[5] Deborah Sontag, "When Politics Is Personal," *New York Times Magazine*, 15 September 2002, p. 90.

lobbying efforts, targeting legislators (and nonpoliticians) who have dealt with cancer as the most likely advocates for funding (Davidson 2002).

There is ample evidence that personal concerns about health-related issues can override a legislator's partisan and ideological commitments. Senator Kay Bailey Hutchison (R-TX) is a no-nonsense Republican, but has shown a strong emotional attachment to cancer funding. Her brother suffered from cancer and underwent a bone marrow transplant and chemotherapy, both difficult experiences. So moved by this experience was Hutchison that she became something of a crusader for cancer funding and a "patient's bill of rights." Her liberal cosponsor, Barbara Mikulski (D-MD), says simply, "She wanted to take a personal situation and turn it into public policy."[6] There are many of examples of legislators who are driven by firsthand health experiences, much like Specter's focus after his brain tumor was discovered. As one report highlighted,

> When Rep. Barbara Vucanovich (R-Colo.) discovered she had breast cancer at age 61, she sponsored legislation that would extend Medicare coverage for mammograms in older women. After Jim Moran (D-Va.) learned that his 3-year-old daughter had a malignant brain tumor, he switched sides on the health insurance debate, and declared that every American should have health benefits. Sen. Strom Thurmond (R-SC) sponsored an alcohol labeling measure after losing his 22-year-old daughter to a drunk driver.[7]

Family histories also shape legislators' identities, which in turn influence their stances toward issues that touch upon those identities. Immigration policies are a prime example. When immigration reform was debated in the Senate, some unlikely supporters of liberalizing immigration emerged on the Republican side of the aisle. Senators Domenici, Specter, Jon Kyl (R-AZ), and Mel Martinez (R-FL) all supported some version of a temporary worker program, and all four told stories of their immigrant ancestors who arrived in the United States decades earlier looking for work.[8]

As these examples show, a legislator's family is a particularly powerful influence. Conservative senator Mike DeWine (R-OH) began pushing for tougher drunk-driving penalties after his 22-year-old daughter was killed in an alcohol-related auto accident in 1993 (Cooper 1996). Congressman Bill Delahunt (D-MA) introduced bills to support oversees adoption. Delahunt adopted a Vietnamese daughter rescued during the fall of Saigon.

Having a child in combat can have profound effects. Congressman Joe Wilson (R-SC) was one of the few legislators with a child serving in the

[6] Janet Battaile, "Public Lives: A Tough Texas Senator is a Crusader against Cancer," *New York Times,* 9 July 2001, p. A8.

[7] Laura Blumenfeld, "When Politics Becomes Personal," *Washington Post,* 19 June 1996, P. C1

[8] Rachel L. Swarns, "An Immigration Debate Framed by Family Ties," *New York Times,* 4 April 2006, p A1.

military as part of combat actions in Iraq. His son Alan was an intelligence officer there during the deadliest months of 2004.

> Often as Wilson . . . sat in lengthy House hearings this year, the soldier's e-mails would arrive on his BlackBerry messaging device, which he would pass down the row to committee colleagues. The short missives about daily life in Iraq often gave Wilson and his colleagues more of a real-world view than they received from the top brass.

Chair of the Armed Service Committee Duncan Hunter (R-CA) was once an Army Ranger and also had a son serving a tour in Iraq as an artillery officer. Perhaps as a result of these experiences, Hunter was one of only two Republicans in the House to oppose the creation of a new intelligence director as recommended by the 9–11 Commission. "He often cites his son's experiences in Iraq for his belief that the change would slow delivery of critical battlefield intelligence to war-fighters on the ground."[9] As powerful as these cases might be, having family in the military is not necessary for personal experience to influence congressional activity. Representative Charlie Wilson (D-TX) was moved by what he observed during World War II and his time in the navy to intervene covertly on behalf of Afghanistan against the Russian military (Crile 2003).

Representative Deborah Pryce (R-OH) has been associated in complicated ways with issues of abortion and child adoption since she entered the House in 1992. Although she served near the top of the House Republican leadership, difficult personal experiences have led her to break with her party on a number of occasions. Pryce's daughter, Caroline, suffered and died from a rare form of cancer in 1999, an event that only strengthened her tenacity on these issues. In additional to her unorthodox approach to abortion issues, at least among Republicans, she "broke party ranks" and voted against the party-supported ban on human cloning in early 2003. Pryce takes actions like these because she views improving the nation's health care system as a central personal goal. Caroline's death and Pryce's divorce at about the same time had tremendous influence on her activities in Washington. As Pryce puts it, "It's not just healthcare and adoption. I don't know; everything I do I probably look at differently."[10] One consequence of a personal encounter with an issue is that it redefines the issue for the legislator.

Experiences are of course more varied than a one-time encounter with a disease or profession. Even generational differences can reveal themselves in patterns of activity. Congressman Richard Neal (D-MA) was or-

[9] Andrea Stone, "For a Few in Congress, War Is a Family Concern," *USA Today,* 6 December 2004.

[10] Jonathan E. Kaplan, "Daughter's Death Changes Pryce's Perspective," *The Hill,* 2 April 2003.

phaned in the 1960s and managed to pay for his college education on the monthly survivor's benefit from Social Security. His generation, he says, is loyal to the program because it was the first to come of age under it. As one reporter put, "Neal's experiences have made him a fierce defender of the traditional Social Security system" at a time when many reform proposals were in the works.[11]

As I will show, religious affiliations can be powerful determinants of policy action. Faith played a surprising role when the Congress impeached and tried President Clinton over the Lewinsky affair. Religious values exerted indirect influence on House members' votes via their party affiliations. Consider the following reflections from two of the four Republicans who voted against all four articles of impeachment.

Representative Peter King (R-NY), a "prototypical 1950s New York Irish kid," offered a personal and strongly religious justification that stems from his strong Catholic background.

> One thing I carry with me is the concept of original sin. . . . None of us is perfect, and we should be careful before pointing the finger at someone else. And because a person has a failing, you don't demonize them. I do feel people, in part, have demonized President Clinton. . . . The president is guilty of weakness, but I never saw him as an evil person.[12]

Christopher Shays (R-CT), a Christian Scientist, reports that he started reading the Bible and praying daily during the week of the impeachment vote. He looked for guidance as to his conduct during the deliberations. It helped him verify that his "motives were right and I could live with the results" and "see the truth as I saw it." Sometimes minor policy matters reflect personal views because party leaders and other actors are uninterested; other times members rely on introspection to make monumental choices when they believe partisanship, ideology, and constituency are insufficient guides.

Religious values are central to debates over the new array of bioethical issues. Catholic members of Congress received heavy media attention when embryonic stem cell research was debated. Many were Democrats whose party supported the research, in apparent contraction of church doctrine. An interesting set on the other side were the five Mormon senators. While just as staunchly antiabortion as many of their Catholic colleagues, they supported stem cell research. Senators Orrin Hatch (R-UT) and Gordon Smith (R-OR), both conservative Republicans, bucked the party line when

[11] Peter S. Canellos, "Lawmaker Finds a Generation Gulf on Social Security," *Boston Globe,* 24 February 2005.

[12] Bill Broadway, "Impeachment Raises Questions of Faith," *Washington Post,* 9 January 1999.

their church suggested that stem cell research might be acceptable. "All five Mormon senators . . . have come out for such funding. They have helped move the debate away from right-to-life absolutism without sacrificing pro-life theology. The LDS Church, not the Vatican, is playing the pivotal role in the struggle over stem cells."[13] Unlike Catholics and evangelicals, Mormons do not believe that life begins at conception. Church doctrine holds that a person lives as a spirit before receiving a physical body, so fertilization itself it not an especially important marker. Indeed, Senator Smith made this precise argument in his testimony supporting embryonic stem cell research.

As Rick Santorum's story in the first chapter illustrated, convictions like these can transform a member who was once a passive participant on an issue to a policy entrepreneur who takes the lead in the policymaking process. As much as personal experiences affect roll call voting, these stories indicate that they might be even more important in spurring a legislator to action. As he tells it, conservative senator Alan Simpson (R-WY) "had no intention of speaking" on the floor when the Senate took up mental health legislation in 1996. But the debate conjured up thoughts of his niece, who had committed a violent suicide. He gave a speech. Said Simpson, "It was in my craw and I had to express it."[14]

Not all cases are this dramatic, but the effects are no less consequential. Sometimes occupational or other expertise shapes legislators' actions. For example, debate over bioengineered food brought representatives' firsthand experiences to the surface. Congressman Nick Smith (R-MI) grew genetically modified soybeans and corn on his farm and believed that they are not only safe but desirable. As chair of the Basic Science Research Subcommittee, Smith authored a report promoting genetically altered crops and opposing government regulation.

The Nurse Reinvestment Act of 2002 was passed into law to address the nursing shortage facing American health care facilities. A number of women in Congress—three of them registered nurses—worked outside the spotlight to make it happen. Senator Debbie Stabenow's (D-MI) mother was a retired nurse. The sympathy for nurses that Stabenow developed watching her mother energized her support for the nursing act. Lois Capps (D-CA), a former public school nurse herself, "would simply not let up on the issue."[15] Her background made her more credible as an advocate for the bill, as did her membership on the Health subcommittee. But nei-

[13] Drew Clark, "The Mormon Stem-Cell Choir," Slate, 3 August 2001. <http://slate.msn.com/?id=112974>

[14] Laura Blumenfeld, "When Politics Becomes Personal," *Washington Post,* 19 June 1996, P. C1

[15] David S. Broder, "The Nursing Bill: A Quiet Triumph," *Washington Post,* 7 August 2002, p. A21.

ther of these facts required her to work as hard as she did on behalf of the legislation. Capps's active participation was yet another case where personal relevance motivated a member of Congress to devote effort to the issue.

In Their Own Words

In addition to these examples from the media, I sought direct evidence from members themselves. To help bolster my confidence in the generalizability of the cases described above, I conducted in-depth interviews with six former members of the House of Representatives. The interviews complement the anecdotes above because they permitted me to probe below the superficial level of newspaper stories and allow members to speak in an open-ended fashion. Because all of these legislators had already left public life, none had reason to spin their responses to make them more palatable to constituents or interest groups. The explanations they offered were not crafted to win my vote. This liberation from electoral and partisan pressures makes former members of Congress an especially attractive source of information. They are an underutilized group who can provide insights into the workings of the institution without being subject to the pressures that current members face (Edwards 2003). I used my discussions with them not just to confirm the scattered anecdotes that show up in media accounts. As a sort of deep background, they also inform my theoretical approach and help generate hypotheses that are tested more systematically in later chapters.

I interviewed former representatives Glenn Browder (D-AL), Bradley Carson (D-OK), Romano Mazzoli (D-KY), Dan Miller (R-FL), Connie Morella (R-MD), and Philip Sharp (D-IN). While such a small sample is not perfectly representative of the House, the members do vary in terms of party, region, and ideology. They vary in longevity, having spent between four and 24 years in the House. They also departed the House by differing means, in some cases years before our interviews and in others just weeks before I met with them. The interviews took place between March 2003 and February 2005 and ranged between 45 and 90 minutes. With permission, I tape-recorded and later transcribed each conversation. The interviews were semistructured: I used the same set of general questions with each member to open the discussion but tailored later questions to the specific situation. The standard questions asked members how they decided to become active, how much their districts influenced them, and on which issues they had a personal interest. In addition to probing the frequency with which personal traits manifested themselves in congressional behavior, the interviews helped ground my theory in real-world politics and suggest more general relationships. As such, the interviews served as "backgrounders" for me in the way that other sources do for journalists. Here I provide some excerpts from these interviews as additional evidence, but our discussions also flavor the entirety of the book even when they are not explicitly cited.

Phil Sharp represented central Indiana as a moderate Democrat. When environmental issues crept onto the agenda during his time in the House, he began to feel pressure from his family in a way that he had not on other matters. As Sharp told me,

> My son, when he became a junior in high school . . . God, he was suddenly, intensely interested in environmental issues and intensely well informed. He was better informed than I was about the individuals and things like that. And I began to realize that when I voted on something environmental, I was going to be quizzed at home. Now I had generally a very good environmental record, but it wasn't 100%.

I asked Brad Carson, who represented western Oklahoma in the House, to explain where his special interest in Native American issues originated. For Carson, it is a family matter that has natural implications for his public life. As he explained,

> My family comes from a rural part of Oklahoma that was settled by the Cherokee Indian tribe that was relocated from southeastern parts of the country. And so my mother is somewhat a part of the Cherokee family. I don't look it much, I'm an eighth. But that's the nature of Indian life in Oklahoma; it's heavily assimilated into the surrounding Anglo, African-American, but increasingly large Latino community. My father was employed in the Bureau of Indian Affairs.

Carson's father worked on a Navajo reservation. Indeed, Carson's family arrived in Oklahoma six generations earlier on the Trail of Tears and was deeply committed to their Native American heritage.

When he took office in 2001, Carson was the third youngest member of the House. Thinking back to Richard Neal's experience with Social Security and the generation gap in Congress, I asked Carson about the role that his age played. Although political scientists rarely speak of these effects in Congress, Carson readily provided a generational assessment of the legislature.

> Today the Congress is run by baby boomers whose formative experiences are of the sixties. And I often said I saw the battle of the sixties being fought out every single day on the House floor. Which side of the issue were you on, where you stood on Vietnam, is where you stood on Iraq. Where you stood on all those social upheavals in the sixties determines were you stood on the cultural matters of the day. And these are the defining things for all the people in Con-

> gress, but for younger members, they aren't defining moments. I came of age when civil rights had largely been resolved, when abortion rights had been resolved, and it didn't have a lot of symbolic importance that they did to older members that didn't take those achievements for granted.

For middle-age members, the Iraq invasion of 2003 resurrected the issues of the Vietnam era, thus coloring their views of its merits and liabilities. Younger members who had only known the 1991 Gulf War and military interventions of the 1980s obviously saw the Iraq conflict differently. Again it seems that legislators' formative experiences framed current policy debates in different ways.

When it comes to reliving the culture wars of the 1960s, Connie Morella offered a different perspective on the same generational distinction. Morella first ran for office after being inspired by the women's movement of the early 1970s. As she explained,

> That whole area of women's issues is one that got a lot of my concentration. It was why I wanted to go to the state legislature. And then I developed it further and said, I can do an awful lot federally on women's issues. But I got started on women's issues because the "women's movement put the movement in me."

Although Morella's Republican Party shifted its positions on such issues while she was in the House, she continued to work on "women's issues" such as abortion, child care, domestic violence, and pay equity that were so important in her formative years. Carson, born 36 years later (and male), did not view abortion as a central political issue for Congress. To him it was a dead issue, having been resolved by the courts before he entered public life. To Morella it continued to be a priority because of her early involvement in the women's movement.

I asked Carson which issues he would have addressed had he remained in the House. At least one of these issues had a clear generational connection. Carson admitted having a personal interest in the open source technology movement.[16]

> Although I didn't sit on a committee where I could have a real lever to make a difference on something, those were intellectual interests of mine. And so, I think there is that kind of natural thing. Again, it's the formative experiences. I came of age very much familiar with the Internet and understanding of its social and political impact, in a way that there are members of Congress who don't use the Internet.

Beyond the generational effects Carson felt, his religious faith was an additional factor in legislative decision-making. As the anecdotal evidence

[16] Open source software allows unrestricted access to source code and is often distributed free of charge. Closed source software, such as most Microsoft products, does not make its source code public and is usually sold commercially.

from the media coverage suggested, religion can be a powerful motivator for members of Congress. I asked Carson about this, particularly President Bush's faith-based initiative legislation (analyzed in chapter 5). I wanted to know why Carson voted against the bill, since it was popular with his Oklahoma constituents. The answer connected to his strong Baptist upbringing. In addition to the clear traditions in his family, Carson was a student at Baylor, a prominent Baptist university. His opposition to mixing church and state via the Bush initiative might have even have lost him votes in a 2004 race for U.S. Senate in Oklahoma.

> Part of the Baptist tradition is—it's been lost in the last 30 years really—but there was a time when Baptists were at the very forefront of church-state separation. And when I was at Baylor that was still a current that was certainly within the students a minority position, but among the faculty and the elite of the university, was a very strong majority position. That's a great example of where being a Baptist influenced me a lot, although probably most Baptist preachers and my fellow congregants would have disagreed with the position. And I think in the Senate race I got bashed for it quite a bit.

Clearly Carson's vote on the faith-based funding bill was not cast with an eye on the voters, or even with his fellow rank-and-file Baptists in Oklahoma. It depended more on his own views about church and state that stemmed from formative experiences as a college student.

Carson's was not the only case where voters' concerns were overridden by their representative's personal views. I asked Ron Mazzoli about his actions on tobacco legislation, an area considered in more depth in chapter 3. Mazzoli's district around Louisville depended on the tobacco industry and, especially at the time before the tobacco wars of the 1990s, was strongly supportive of big tobacco and crop farming more generally.[17] Yet Mazzoli decided to take on the industry despite his constituents' views. As Mazzoli recalled, his action emerged from personal concerns about tobacco advertising aimed at children.

> I remember doing a piece on the House floor, one of those special orders where you can take a fair amount of time to develop your point. I had something that sort of suggested what the research was showing was that a lot of young people were being enticed into smoking because you had Joe Camel . . . and I just really thought that they were being duplicitous about their advertising techniques. They were saying that they only targeted grown-ups and they were dissuading young people from smoking, but I didn't think that was the case.

The tobacco industry was not happy with the congressman's complaints about their advertising practices, and Mazzoli knew it. The opposition

[17] Until his decision in the 1990s not to accept PAC contributions, FEC records show that Mazzoli took at least $10,700 from tobacco PACs between 1977 and 1988.

from his district and beyond was predictable, but Mazzoli's convictions were more important than the backlash. He recalled that

> in addition to having the tobacco workers, and some members of the machinists who were doing the work manufacturing the tobacco, you had the Farm Bureau Federation, which in Kentucky is extremely strong. We had other organized labor that, because of solidarity, it may not have been directly involved in tobacco, but because of solidarity, felt that they had to weigh in on this issue against me on behalf of their brethren in the movement. So it was a very tough situation.

I asked Mazzoli why he chose to get out front on this issue rather than simply cast a quiet roll call vote in favor of tobacco regulation, which interest groups and voters might not have noticed so much.

> Some would say, well, it's from a rigid Catholic upbringing. You have some of this stuff drummed into you by the sisters and the brothers and the parochial school from grade school through college. But, some would say, it's from your mother and father trying to teach you what's right and wrong and that they never had much of anything. My dad was an immigrant and never got out of grade school, but was a very hardworking man. My mother was a high school graduate who worked with him.

The lessons he learned from his parents' diligence were not about tobacco at the time, but they resonated when he observed what seemed to be improper practices in the tobacco industry. He continued,

> They didn't have life easy. They were not hardscrabble, but it was a tough life. They had to make a payroll for their little company. I always saw them doing the right thing and sometimes suffering as a result of doing the right thing of being honest.

Tobacco was a lesser issue in Mazzoli's career, but nonetheless one on which he took political heat to fulfill a personal motivation. Mazzoli's greatest legislative legacy is his work on immigration, having coauthored the 1986 Immigration Reform and Control Act, which liberalized and rationalized immigration barriers. It sounds like an unusual issue for a Kentucky congressman to raise given his district and the times. Why would the representative of a politically conservative and largely white district pursue an accommodating immigration policy that most of his constituents would likely oppose? His Italian surname told the story.

> I'd say that first of all, my dad's being an immigrant and my mother having been a daughter of immigrants, that certainly did open me up. It certainly did lay a foundation for my working in this issue and to have some views on it.

But like Santorum in his approach to abortion policy, Mazzoli did not tackle immigration immediately after being elected to the House. "So," Mazzoli asked rhetorically, "the question is why would I, and by that time, pretty much into my career, would have chosen immigration." The answer depends on both his immigrant roots and his Catholic education at Notre Dame. The issue came to Mazzoli

> because Father Hesburgh, the president of Notre Dame University, who became president when I was a sophomore there back in 1952, was ending two years of work as chair of Jimmy's Carter immigration reform panel. And they were about to yield a magnum opus and Father Ted knew that this—or felt with the impressions that he's possessed his lifetime—was correct in saying that this was an issue with legs. This was going to be some issue that wasn't going to be just a temporal thing.

Hesburgh made an impression on Mazzoli then and continued to counsel him during the rest of his congressional tenure. Mazzoli explained that he viewed himself as a vehicle for Father Hesburgh's policy concerns.

> He really wanted people he thought who had balance, and obviously people who might have some connection with Notre Dame, to be involved in the issue. . . . So, anyway, long and short of it, because of his discussion with me, phone calls and so forth, I decided . . . against the best of my political judgment . . . to take the committee.

Personal experiences like these have the potential to trump constituent and partisan preferences not only on roll call votes but even on more consequential, proactive behavior.

As the media examples suggested, family health issues can change a member's position and agenda overnight. For Dan Miller, it was his son's problematic blood condition and subsequent organ transplant that gave these issues special priority. Miller stated matter-of-factly, "I was interested in hemophilia. My son was a hemophiliac. He was cured when he had a liver transplant." This experience moved Miller to focus legislation on blood and liver diseases, raising the issue whenever possible. He explained that

> hemophilia is a fairly rare disease, and so I would have language in the bill so that they [the National Institutes of Health] knew about hemophilia. When they came to testify before the committee, they would talk about hemophilia. Hemophilia otherwise had a hard time getting any attention at NIH.

Like so many other health issues, the issue created strange bedfellows, of which Miller was one. Advocates of liver disease research often turned to him for access and support for their cause.

> I remember after my son was having liver problems, when the liver people call for an appointment, they got an appointment with me. They couldn't have had an appointment without it. So, it gave you a reason and motivation to get involved. And Steve Lynch [a freshman Democratic congressman from Massachusetts who donated half of his liver to an ill brother-in-law] got involved. We together cosponsored a bill, Democrat and Republican, to push the issue.

I asked Glenn Browder about the factors he considered in supporting the Americans with Disabilities Act (ADA) of 1990. The ADA guaranteed new forms of access for disabled citizens and thus placed some new burdens on companies to comply. The business community in his Alabama district was opposed to what they perceived as the ADA's costly mandates. Browder's firsthand experience with a developmentally delayed family member proved more important than the pressure of business interests. He recalled that "in terms of the ADA, I thought about my [disabled] nephew. He was 20-something at that time. Obstacles that he has, and his family have—they are not well to do. Working class is one of the problems that he has." The vivid memory of his nephew defined Browder's framing of the issue. As he put it,

> I don't want to call it the "relative imperative" or the "kinship imperative," but as soon as you're into it, it made me think of it in terms of, I guess, personal ways as opposed to just, What's this going to cost? Or what are the benefits of this going to be to society? It made me think of it in personal—personalized it for me.

Browder did not live an easy life himself. His challenging upbringing colored everything he did on Capitol Hill, although it was more evident in some cases than others. He explained to me that it guided the nominations he made to the military service academies such as West Point.[18] His philosophy was that people in difficult situations only needed an opportunity to succeed, and he could help provide it.

> I grew up very poor. I'm not campaigning for office today, so I'm not making my "poor boy speech," but very, very poor. My father died in jail when I was one year old. My mother had a second-grade education. My stepfather had a third-grade education, I think. Six of us lived on the wrong side of town and worked in the mill. I'm the first person I knew even went to high school or graduated from high school.

Those experiences stuck with him. "That's always with me—I've always cared about greatly. And when I would look at the academy, I'd keep an eye out for qualified people who didn't have the advantages."

[18] Members of Congress have the authority to nominate candidates to each of the five national military service academies.

As the only female member I interviewed, Connie Morella, reflected on her experiences as a mother and caregiver. When her sister died of breast cancer, Morella became the legal guardian of six nieces and nephews along with three children of her own. She became an advocate of subsidized child-care for federal workers after watching her then-adult children struggle to balance work outside the home and care for their children, her grandchildren. Her energy on the issue led to the creation of the Child Care Caucus in House. As she saw it, "the child care issue, the whole caucus" came from those experiences.

> I even went to the White House. Whole child-care issues, and child support issues, too . . . knowing my kids, who are now married. One of them is a nurse, and another one is a teacher. And even though they were home when [their children] were really tiny, now that they're starting school, they still have to work out issues for child care.

Her efforts to support federal child care were targeted at people just like her daughters because she used knowledge of their life experiences to inform her policy choices.

The issue most associated with Dan Miller's tenure in the House is statistical sampling in the 2000 census. In advance of the 2000 enumeration, the Census Bureau considered augmenting the "hard count" with statistical sampling to estimate the number of people not counted. Research had shown that minority and low-income individuals were most likely to be missed, so sampling was proposed to remedy the disproportionate undercount. The Republicans opposed sampling on the grounds that it violated the Constitution's requirement to conduct an "actual enumeration" of the population. Almost by accident, Miller says, he became the Republican Party's point person in the fight against statistical sampling. Miller has a Ph.D. in statistics and was a professor at Georgia State University before entering the House.

> Even though I taught statistics," he explained to me, "I really never studied the details of the Census. I've never considered myself a Census person; I do statistics. And I haven't taught it for 20-some years. But, when the issue started becoming critical . . . all of a sudden the issue of adjustment came up and so it became a big issue with Newt Gingrich, the Speaker, and Denny Hastert, who was then chairman of the subcommittee.

How then did Miller become the point person on the Census?

> We were debating something on the floor and I went down there and one of the things I used to use was a little book called *How to Lie with Statistics*. It's kind of a fun little book, and I used to use that for my first lecture in statistics. On the first day they're not very prepared, and it was just kind of a get-their-

> attention. So, I started talking about that one time on the floor of the House. And Denny Hastert heard something about statistics, and so they specifically asked me to chair a new subcommittee.

Miller spent the next several years successfully opposing Democratic proposals to introduce statistical adjustments to the census enumeration.

I asked members whether their previous careers or other expertise outside the House motivated assignments to particular committees in this way. For example, one might expect a former farmer to be naturally interested in a seat on the Agriculture Committee. This might happen out of personal concern or because related experience would make the transition to the committee easier. Contrary to some of the literature on committee assignments and my expectations, the members I interviewed often did the opposite. Morella, being a former teacher and having raised a total of nine children, might have naturally gravitated to the House Education Committee. But Morella purposely avoided the committee.

> The reason I didn't choose to be on the Education Committee was because I was an educator. I thought, "Hey, I want to go into something else," because I always was able to—I hope—call on my experiences as an educator. And you know, my kids all went to public schools, so I'd watch that very closely. But I just felt that I could do more on another committee.

I asked Phil Sharp, a former college professor, why he did not seek out a slot on Education and got the same response. "Those things in my background always came into play in my ability to talk about things, in my ability to deal with them back home, so it's not like they were dead. Like with education, I was able to talk about things." Both Morella and Sharp took assignments on other committees assuming that they could weigh in on education issues because of their background. These cases suggest that a representative's committee assignments do not define the full range of issues on which she will be active.

These interviews deepen the understanding of personal characteristics that media accounts suggested. In some cases, such as Miller's statistics background, an experience shapes activity on just one issue. But in other cases, such as Morella's experience as a mother or Carson's generational orientation, their personal traits seem to have a pervasive effect on how they act across a range of issues. As Mazzoli's experiences on tobacco and immigration made clear, there were instances in which these personal interests transcended the concerns of their constituencies. In the following section, I demonstrate in a more systematic way that members' voting records do indeed diverge from their constituents' preferences. In a later section, I will propose that legislators' personal motivations exaggerate this divergence when more proactive forms of lawmaking are considered.

How Much Representation?

Responsiveness to the interests of constituents is a central demand in any democratic political system. The dominance of the substantive representation focus in congressional scholarship is testimony to its assumed importance. Because we operate in a republican system, the national legislature is considered the primary institution for representing constituents. Scrutiny of empirical evidence finds substantial correspondence between a district's preferences and legislators' votes, yet there is also good evidence that full policy representation does not occur. For one, correlation is not the same as causation, and constituent pressure is only one of many forces acting on legislators. Accordingly, one should not assume for theoretical purposes that legislators' actions always reflect district preferences. Thus, my inquiry starts merely by assessing the degree to which representatives' actions deviate from their constituents' wishes. Later I shall identify the causes of discord over policy between constituents and representatives. Failure to explore the sources of slack between representatives and the represented is one of the most serious weaknesses of the recent scholarly literature.

Researchers have devoted great effort to understanding the impact of ideology, parties, and interest groups on roll call voting, but rarely have personal factors been considered as independent variables, or legislative activities other than voting been studied as dependent variables. The reason seems to be that under the current methodological paradigm legislators appear highly responsive to voters' policy concerns, leaving little room for other factors. A number of studies now demonstrate that representatives usually act in ways that are consistent with constituents' wishes (Ansolabehere, Snyder, and Stewart 2001a; Burden 2004a; Erikson and Wright 2000; Jackson and King 1989). This means that the positions legislators take on policy nicely correspond with the expressed preferences of constituents in their districts. Although correspondence is a measure of policy responsiveness, it is not evidence of a causal relationship (Achen 1978; Bernstein 1989). Without a full causal model, we cannot rule out the possibility that much representation is coincidental (Hill and Hinton-Anderson 1995). Much of the connection between a district's preferences and its legislator's actions is coincidental, as I will argue later. For now we shall take a strong relationship between those preferences and legislators' positions as a sign of robust policy representation, whether driven by voters' requiring accountability or, more likely, other causes.

I examine this relationship for one recent Congress as an illustration of the kind of evidence that is frequently employed in the literature. I take a member's first dimension DW-NOMINATE score as a measure of his roll call voting positions. Recall that NOMINATE uses nearly all of the roll call votes cast in a Congress to place members on a continuum from most liberal (−1) to most conservative (+1) and is often viewed as an indicator of ideology. To measure district preferences, I use the share of the two-party presidential vote cast in each district for Republican George W. Bush in 2000, so that higher values also indicate greater conservatism. Although not a perfect measure of a district's preferences, the closely fought election of 2000 provides a useful benchmark for assessing the left-right tendencies of constituents. The NOMINATE data come from the 106th House, which was in session during the 2000 election campaign. If legislators' votes reflect district ideological preferences, there should be strong positive association between the two measures.

A scatterplot of these two measures appears in figure 2.1. Each dot indicates a legislator-district dyad. The data clearly run upward from left to right, indicating a positive relationship between district preferences and legislator positions. The dots are also concentrated in two clumps, one for the Democrats in the lower left quadrant and one for the Republicans in the upper right quadrant. This suggests that a representative's party membership must be an intervening variable between voter preferences and her actions, if not a determinant of her ideology itself. The fact that districts are roughly normally distributed while legislators are bimodal hints that legislative partisanship might actually be inhibiting, not enhancing, representation.

The point of the figure is to show that representation is robust yet far from perfect, a point that has recently been made elsewhere (Clinton 2006) but was also revealed in earlier empirical studies of representation (Erikson, Mackuen, and Stimson 2002; Miller and Stokes 1963). The overall correlation between district preferences and representatives' votes is .74. Even though it is one of the strongest relationships in recent years, it suggests that district ideological preferences only explain about half of the positioning by incumbents ($R^2 = .74^2 = .55$). Moreover, the correlation is even weaker within parties. For the Democrats it is .68 and for Republicans it is .45. Within parties the variance in voting behavior explained within a party is between 20% and 45%. Examining earlier Congresses would exhibit even less explanatory power. Obviously much is left to explain after one has considered constituency and party affiliation.

It would thus be a mistake to automatically equate legislators' preferences with constituents' preferences. Even as an implied formal modeling abstraction (Krehbiel 1991), it violates the data to a degree that is unacceptable. District preferences appear to be an important correlate of legislators' positions, but they remain theoretically and empirically distinct. As Bianco frames the situation, "Scholars may wish to evaluate legislatorial behavior in terms of constituent interest, but they cannot assume that these interests directly influence behavior" (1992, 156). A fairer assessment of

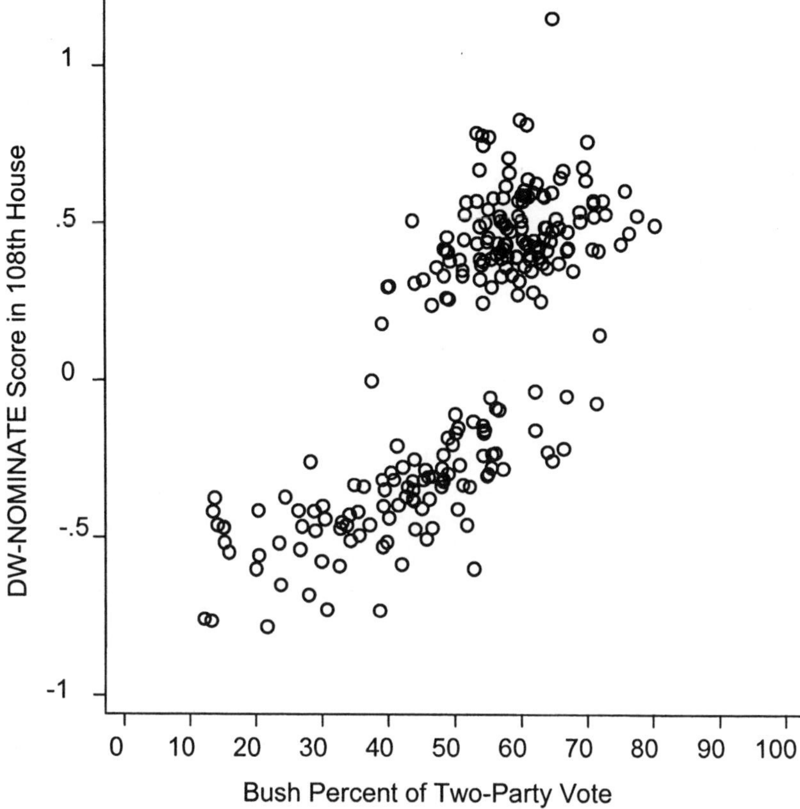

Figure 2.1. Representation in the 106th House of Representatives

congressional preferences is needed that more explicitly seeks their origins. If district ideology can account for at best half of the variation in roll call voting patterns, what else influences congressional behavior? To better understand why legislators do what they do and to evaluate the health of the democratic system, one must first unpack the sources of congressional preferences. I argue that constituents' preferences can have but a limited influence on what legislators do.

Elections and Monitoring

James Madison reasoned in the Federalist Papers that elections would be the mechanism that would keep legislators honest and accountable to their constituents. Though they are not angels, elected officials nonetheless heed public opinion for fear of being defeated when they seek reelection. Some observers might even reason that elections are the *only* way for constituents to ensure that representatives comply with their wishes. While elections are critical to ensuring policy representation, I suggest that the reasons are not those that Madison supposed. To be specific, I assert that elections are not particularly effective in using fear as a tool to motivate recalcitrant legislators to adopt more acceptable positions.

Why do voters not force their views on their representatives? First, we have already noted that the principal-agent relationship is imperfect. The principals—constituents—lack the information and other resources needed to monitor their representatives. It is impossible for a voter to track every bill introduced, speech given, and statement made by his representative, let alone the hundreds of roll call votes that occur each year. It is of course possible that constituents are uninterested most of the time, but that segments of the public become attentive when issues salient to them are addressed. Interest groups or other opinion leaders could alert voters when a policy of concern to them is being altered. Rather than expressed opinion, preferences lying latent in the district might motivate responsiveness to the district (Arnold 1990; Hutchings 2003; Miller and Stokes 1963). However intriguing this view, the process it identifies cannot have much effect beyond a small number of highly visible roll call votes. A key reason is the general lack of serious competition in congressional elections.

Second, legislators purposely create conditions that give them latitude on policy. Fenno (1978) described the stylistic process by which legislators build up constituent trust, which in turn creates voting leeway (see also Arnold 1990; Bianco 1994; Hibbing 1991). As noted in chapter 1, the absence of competition in congressional elections dampens the electoral imperative as a motivation for faithful behavior by the agent. Only incumbents can provide pork and other constituent services, thus discouraging the best challengers at the outset (Fiorina 1989; Mayhew 1974). The result is that many challengers who do run are inexperienced and unprepared for a serious campaign (Jacobson 2004). Parker (1992) proposes that members of Congress are in fact discretion-maximizing; they value the policy freedom that safe seats provide. By building up incumbent advantages, they ward off competition and take advantage of the monopoly the office provides. Incumbents seldom face opponents with enough resources and credibility to point out failed agency. Thus, both the difficulty of monitoring and the lack of quality challengers make elections poor tools for inducing responsiveness among incumbents to the preferences of their constituents.

Elections nonetheless hold the power to affect representation, but the effects are felt more on election day itself than during interelection governing periods. Rather than monitor and guide stray incumbents, voters are more likely to be well represented if they select candidates at the outset who share their values. Because slack exists and can be filled in part by representatives' own wishes, it is most effective to exert influence at the "selection" stage rather than the "persuasion" stage, by choosing legislators who already agree with constituents, at least on some key issues (Fearon 1999; Fordham and McKeown 2003). Candidate recruitment thus becomes a critical part of representation. As Kingdon discovered, "That the recruitment process affects congressmen's voting is an elemental, easy-to-understand proposition, but its profound importance cannot be emphasized too strongly" (1989, 46).

Acknowledging this reality helps explain why policy change occurs primarily by replacement rather than conversion (Asher and Weisberg 1978; Brady and Sinclair 1984; Poole and Rosenthal 1997; Rohde 1991). Replacing a member, even with another member of the same party, often results in dramatic changes in voting record even though the constituency's views remain more or less fixed (Brady and Linn 1973). This is exactly what the comparison of Santorum and Specter in Chapter 1 demonstrated. The two senators from Pennsylvania are unlikely to moderate their views on abortion and stem cell research regardless of public opinion. Dissatisfied Keystone State voters would be more likely to see their views represented by replacing a senator than pressuring the one they have.

The available evidence already demonstrates that representatives' policy positions have at best modest effects on their electoral fortunes. Canes-Wrone, Brady, and Cogan (2002) find that even a shift of 25 points on the Americans for Democratic Action (ADA) 100-point scale would only alter a given member's vote share by two or three percentage points and affect the likelihood of holding a safe seat (defined as winning over 60% of the vote) by six points. Although this might sound like a substantial effect, we should keep two facts in mind that limit the likelihood of observing this very often.

First, House reelection rates hover above 90%, so even a 10-point change in a legislator's vote score would not add much risk. Election outcomes are greatly affected by incumbents' constituent service, success in directing pork barrel spending to the district, and preemptive fund-raising. This leaves relatively little room for policy to have an effect. Second, few members change their voting patterns enough to move a quarter of the way down the ADA scale (Poole and Rosenthal 1997). Hinich and Munger (1994) point out that politicians' reputations constrain them from changing positions dramatically. I have argued that excessive movement can cost a legislator as many votes as are gained by moderating his position (Burden 2004a). The effects of moderations that I estimate are amazingly similar to Canes-Wrone, Brady, and Cogan: a shift of 20 points toward the center on a 101-point ideological scale adds about two percentage points to a candidate's vote share. In a close race, a couple of percentage points matter a great deal, but such elections are few and far between in the U.S. Congress. Monitoring and direct control of legislators between elections are thus not sufficient to ensure policy representation. Since these actions are the backbone of principal-agent theory, one can only conclude that substantial slack exists between the preferences of constituents and the actions of their representatives.

The Origins of Preferences

The discussion thus far pushes us to the question of the sources of legislative preferences. Legislators' voting records correspond to district ideology only roughly, even less once party affiliation is taken into account. Monitoring and electoral threat are not especially powerful means for inducing policy compliance since incumbents do not bear much cost for deviating from voter preferences. If constituents cannot force an elected official to internalize their preferences fully, then what are the origins of representatives' positions?

Although Krehbiel's (1991) information theory of legislation organization is presented as a rebuttal of Shepsle and Weingast's (1987) distributive model, they seem to share one monumental but often implicit assumption: legislators' preferences are derived from the median voters in their districts. The ongoing debate about whether committees are staffed with "preference outliers" does not challenge the first premise, present in both models, that legislators internalize the wishes of their constituents. Opening up the black box of preferences not only refocuses the recent congressional literature but transcends debates that have swept their common assumptions under the rug.

There is no doubt that a representative is influenced by many forces in his environment. The factors thought to affect legislators' actions have largely been catalogued by the existing literature. A landmark study, Kingdon's *Congressmen's Voting Decisions,* alerted researchers to the fact that a legislator must monitor many influences in the environment when facing a roll call vote. The "field of forces," as Kingdon called it, includes six actors: the constituency, fellow members, party leaders, interest groups, the administration, and staff. Fortunately for the legislator, the "field of forces" usually does not suffer from conflict. That is, much of the time most of the forces push a legislator in the same direction. This congruence naturally makes it difficult to isolate the roles played by each factor.

When conflict erupts among the forces, the interview evidence suggests that members tend to consult their House colleagues for advice. Yet Kingdon rightly discounts this as a causal relationship, noting that members tend to "shop" among their colleagues for voting advice that conforms with their predispositions. This rationale could explain why in Kingdon's study members never listed themselves as influences, why the six forces are all external to the representative. It appears from Kingdon's work that legislators are subject entirely to sources outside of their own predilections (aside from established "voting histories" that were presumably a result of the same influences, just at an earlier time). I suspect that members often rely on their own gut feelings, instincts, and experiences and, if convenient, can provide cover from other sources. While Kingdon opens the possibility at the end of the book that "congressmen themselves hold their own attitudes on questions of public policy, and . . . these attitudes affect their votes" (1989, 265), he just as quickly dismisses this possibility.

Following Kingdon's lead, other researchers have assembled lists of the influences on congressional behavior. Lamb's (1998) study of Senators Dick Lugar (R-IN) and Paul Sarbanes (D-MD) identifies six influences. Among these the three "personal" influences are personality, ideology, and policy preferences and are found within the legislator himself. "External" influences are constituency, party, and political context. In a similar vein, Evans's (2002) study of Senate decision-making identified six roll call touchstones: constituency, advocacy groups, partisanship, fellow senators, and "core attitudes and political values." The latter are "less and visible and concrete than are other touchstones" (278). Similar lists appear in Page et al. (1984) and elsewhere in the literature.

The difficulty lies not in creating lists of possible influences but in isolating them empirically. In his analysis of senators' voting records, Levitt (1997) treated ADA scores as a weighted function of constituent preferences, the senator's personal preferences, the preferences of the senator's electoral supporters, and party pressure (see also Carson and Oppenheimer 1984). Although all four factors played some role, personal preferences or "ideology" carried most of the weight. Less than a quarter of the total weight in the decision calculus could be accounted for by voters' preferences. While Levitt's study did not account for all possible influences, it reminds us of the incomplete role played by district opinion that I highlighted earlier.

Other studies also found district preferences to have only a modest impact. Miller and Stokes' seminal study of constituency influence revealed that in fact "the Representative's roll call behavior is strongly influenced by his own policy preferences and by his perception of preferences held by the constituency" (1963, 56). Across the three issue areas examined, neither the standard trustee nor delegate model adequately described the dynamic. The precise relationship between the constituency and the representative was not easily characterized since it "depends very much on the issue involved" (56).[19] Sensitivity to voters' concerns is thus far from uniform.

Although every close study of legislative decision-making admits that multiple forces act on the representative and that personal factors are among them, each hits a dead end in trying to demonstrate that personal views shape legislators' action. For example, in attempting to disaggregate roll call voting data, Uslaner (1999) updates earlier work and finds almost no role for personal ideology or values. As he summarizes, "Legislators don't exercise their own judgment as much as they reflect the multiple constituencies they represent. Not one senator has a pure personal partisanship that qualifies as a 'shirker'" (91). Uslaner's contribution thus points us back to the multiple constituencies arguments of Fenno, Fiorina, and others as explanations for behavior that deviates from the delegate standard (Bishin 2000). While this is a step toward unpacking legislative preferences, it still perceives legislators essentially as robots who happen to act as agents for several constituencies rather than a single median voter.

The approach used by Levitt, Uslaner, and others assumes that personal preferences can be gleaned from roll call votes by "subtracting out" other influences. Yet this single-minded focus on floor votes itself has been subject to serious criticism. Jackson and Kingdon (1992) argue that is all but impossible to disentangle the factors that drive voting patterns, particularly personal ideology since it is often measured with roll call voting data as well. McCarty, Poole, and Rosenthal (2001) point out the possibility of selection effects: roll call scores are partly an artifact of the party a candidate chooses to affiliate with when she first runs for office. Van Doren (1990) offers a more sweeping critique of voting studies, noting that they fail to consider the massive agenda effects that determine which bills will be considered. This is yet another selection bias. Examining a large number of votes, as NOMINATE does, may alleviate this concern, but it also takes the researcher away from policy specifics, which I argue are central to the relationship between constituents and representatives.

A fortunate constituent is represented at the outset by a legislator with views similar to his. Where legislators and constituents have common values, representation happens somewhat automatically, with neither monitoring nor electoral fear being necessary for compliance. Despite the discretion that members enjoy, correspondence between the positions of representatives and voters is not in jeopardy. As Parker contends, much representation is due to shared values between constituents and their repre-

[19] Various authors have revisited the Miller and Stokes dataset. Some find that the original study understated the degree of policy representation (Erikson 1978; Hill and Hurley 1999) but others find the opposite (Achen 1978; Cnudde and McCrone 1966).

sentatives. "Thus, when legislators are expressing their own views and exercising discretion, they are also expressing the views that are dominant within their districts without explicitly attempting to do so" (1992, 106–7; see also Bernstein 1989). To ensure that a representative is faithful, constituents are better off choosing someone like themselves than changing a legislator with different views. Descriptive representation can lead to substantive representation.

Representatives arrive in office with their own ideologies. Some members hold their ideologies more closely than others, but most politicians nonetheless have political philosophies that at least loosely guide their actions. To the degree that these ideologies are public knowledge and voters use them to select candidates, candidates' orientations will correspond to those of their districts. But correspondence cannot be perfect on every issue. On issues such as abortion policy a representative will face a divided constituency that cannot be satisfied with a single position. On other issues constituents will have ill-formed preferences, making it difficult if not impossible to follow public opinion. This ambiguity and the leeway that incumbency creates allow space in which the legislator may rely on introspective representation. And because serving in Congress is about more than just voting on roll calls, members have the opportunity to realize their own views by proactive participation.

Politicians come to office with abstract views—whether they are called philosophies or policy orientations—about which direction government ought to move, to the left or to the right. But ideology is just one of several factors that comprise a legislator's preferences. I suggest three additional items, each of which has been studied extensively at the level of the individual citizen.

First are the representative's values. By values I mean the moral convictions or principles people carry with them. In the study of citizen attitudes, values are understood to be central to an individual's orientation toward politics (Alvarez and Brehm 2002; Feldman 1988; Hochschild 2001; Lane 1962; Rokeach 1973). These values are often religious in nature and thus differ from ideologies. They do not necessarily conform to the left-right spectrum and are not relevant to every issue. An ideology dictates policy prescriptions and provides a general framework for approaching issues; values lie a step deeper in a person's thinking. Values are often acquired earlier in life, derive from forces largely outside of party politics, and tend to be more idiosyncratic.

Values are often consistent with ideologies at a general level, but on specific policies there can be conflict. An example would be faithful Catholics who oppose both abortion and the death penalty, making them neither liberal nor conservative across these two issues. For many politicians, values are selective but intense, while ideologies are comprehensive but tepid. An ideological conservative might generally oppose the expansion of government spending, but might strongly favor it on a small number of issues central to her values. A deep personal experience can sharpen one's values, increasing their intensity and narrowing their aim.

A second source of personal preferences derives from information or prior expertise (Goren 2004; Zaller 1992). Legislators come to office knowing things about policy domains that their colleagues and constituents do not. It is often personal knowledge or experience with an issue that motivate an interest in politics in the first place (Verba, Schlozman, and Brady 1995). In the contemporary era, many candidates run for office having been prosecutors, insurance salesmen, teachers, small business owners, or military service members. Even before being assigned to a committee and becoming a policy specialist, as the House structure requires, most legislators have special information about one or more policy areas. A former trial court judge knows more about sentencing guidelines than does the typical member, and a former teacher has ready expertise on curriculum reform and the effects of student-teacher ratios on student performance. But it is not just occupations that provide information. Having a spouse or other family member engaged in a policy area provides expertise indirectly. I identified many members who suffered health concerns, either personally or via friends and family, and quickly became experts on the afflictions, treatments, and funding. These firsthand (and secondhand) experiences provide information that is not to be discounted.

Third, and typically least important, is self-interest. We say that self-interest is operative when a person pursues goals that favor his own status, advantage, or pleasure (Campbell 2002; Citrin and Green 1990; Feldman 1982; Green and Gerken 1989). Self-interest differs from other forces acting on legislators in a number of ways. Theoretically, self-interest is more personal and less principled than forces like ideology and constituent preferences and so raises serious normative concerns. Empirically, it is more difficult to observe, and its influence on policymaking is probably underestimated in the literature as a result (cf., McGuire and Ohsfeldt 1989). This combination is undesirable because it suggests that researchers are neglecting one of the influences that packs the greatest normative punch. While public decisions are often analyzed in terms of the effect they have on personal behavior, the creeping influence of personal matters on public life is more intriguing.

We have thus noted at least four ways in which factors internal to the legislator will influence his behavior. Values, information, self-interest, and ideology are critical to all human decision-making. Although legislators face other pressures as well, these personal factors can be quite powerful. While the shirking literature has emphasized the degree of slack between district preferences and legislators' votes, it has failed to explore the reasons for slack. Here I have identified several possibilities, each of which carries its own normative baggage. Although I will wait to address these normative concerns until the book's conclusion, it should be clear already that a legislator who disobeys her constituency out of self-interest is normatively quite different from one who does so because of occupational expertise.

A Model of Legislator Action

Representatives' "preferences" have many sources. A rough distinction we have already suggested is whether the origins are internal or external. Among external forces, preferences could be induced by constituent opinion, under the assumption that positions are chosen to increase one's reelection chances, itself a form of self-interested action (Mayhew 1974). Preferences might be also be induced by other principals such as parties, interest groups, or the administration. Among internal forces, they could be genuine policy positions that reflect the perceived public interest, perhaps in the form of an ideology or philosophy. Note that these sources of preferences need not be incompatible. For example, a representative in favor of a "flat" income tax might personally benefit from a regressive system of taxation while believing that it is the right policy on principle. A legislator who enjoys hunting might oppose restrictions on gun ownership for reasons other than her desire to retain arms (Van Dunk 1998). Because the "field of forces" is so often in agreement, disentangling personal and other factors is a tricky business.

Formal models usually treat tastes as given. All preferences are treated equally, with no ambivalence or competition between them and without regard for their origins. This simplifying approach can be quite productive in establishing predictions about actors who have fixed ideal points. But if one of our aims is to render normative judgments about the value of legislators' actions, it matters whether the tastes and behaviors of political actors are based on abstract ideologies, strategies to pacify constituents and activists, information, values, or something else. While summarizing all of these factors in a single ideal point for each actor is useful in a formal model, this study seeks to disentangle them to unpack the sources of preferences and understand why a representative prefers the policies he does. Indeed, several of my theoretical propositions could be easily incorporated into a formal theoretic account, since they detail the conditions under which legislators will act on internal versus external forces, and when they will remain passive rather than active participants in the legislative process.

To summarize, I propose a general model to explain individual legislators' behavior. The model emphasizes personal factors, not necessarily because they are most important but because they have been most neglected by existing scholarship. The model theoretically applies to all types of political actors, though I shall consider it with reference to elected representatives in congress. A diagram of the model appears in figure 2.2. The arrows indicate paths of influence between variables. The main causal path of interest has traditionally been that between *preferences* and *actions,* and it remains the ultimate object of focus in my framework as well. I expand the usual notion of actions beyond mere roll call voting to distinguish between proactive and reactive behavior. On the left side of the figure are the four personal factors that contribute to these preferences: *information, values, self-interest,* and *ideology.* Although many of these are idiosyncratic, depending as they do on personal experiences, I show in ensuing chapters that in many cases they may be measured empirically using data on members' backgrounds and other personal characteristics. These traits influence preferences, which in turn lead to actions. For legislators these actions include roll call votes, but also more proactive behaviors such as making speeches, cosponsoring bills, and persuading other legislators.

Actions are not determined by internal preferences alone. A legislator can be persuaded to adopt positions or take actions different from those she would take based on her own views. I denote any effort by an external principal to affect legislative behavior as *lobbying*. By promising rewards or threatening punishments, actors in the legislators' field of forces can push him to adopt new views or at least take different actions. These principals include parties and interest groups, who tend to do conscious and explicit lobbying, as well as voters, who are typically less attentive but may also exert influence on a legislator, even without consciously trying to do so. Constituents can be more direct by threatening to vote against a representative who acts contrary to their wishes, although I have suggested that even this form of lobbying is not especially powerful. Finally, I use the term *persuasion* to mean either temporary or lasting change in preferences as the result of lobbying. Persuasion does not occur when lobbying results in a change in behavior without an accompanying change in preferences.

To take a particularly prominent form of lobbying, consider the influence of parties on rank-and-file legislators. Party leaders can exert pressure on members by promising rewards such as campaign funds or committee assignments in exchange for support. Although the task is difficult (Krehbiel 1993b), it is clear that parties influence roll call voting and other legislative behavior (Ansolabehere, Snyder, and Stewart 2001b; Binder, Lawrence, and Maltzman 1999; Burden and Frisby 2004; Cox and McCubbins 1993, 2005; Rohde 1991; Snyder and Groseclose 2000). Rather than add another comment on the debate about whether congressional

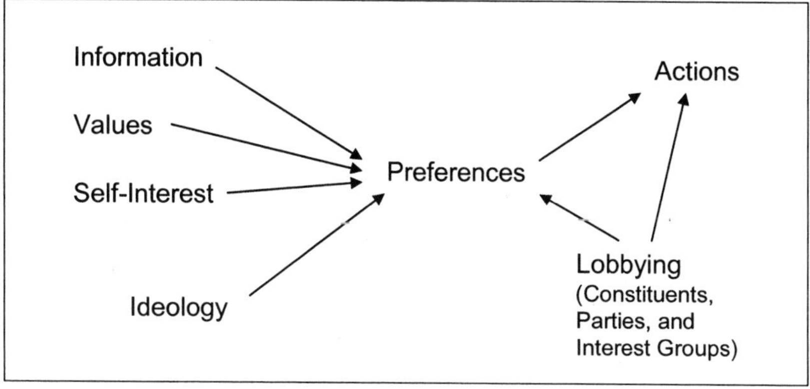

Figure 2.2. A model of legislative behavior

parties "matter," I will argue that a member's party affiliation conditions the effects of personal traits on legislative action. I remain somewhat silent on the specific role played by parties general, instead showing how variables influence behavior differently across the parties.

Disentangling personal interests from other preferences is theoretically important but practically difficult. One's view of the "good society," especially for elites, often reinforces their personal interests, so there is rarely a contradiction between a philosophy or ideology and selfishness. This conjecture is similar to Kingdon's (1989) finding that most forces—interest groups, party leaders, constituents, colleagues, and personal preferences—tend to push a member of Congress in the same voting direction. The task for researchers is to identify policy areas where personal motivations are distinct from these other influences.

In the race among these various forces, there are several reasons why legislators' personal experiences might on occasion rise to the top. Legislation is complex and requires simplification. Many bills contain arcane legal language, deal with technical subject matter, are lengthy, and are moving targets, being constantly revised so that members rarely have the luxury of studying the version they must confront on the floor. As Kingdon showed, members turn to shortcuts, voting cues such as party leaders and fellow members. But this is not a complete solution, nor is it pursued in all cases. In many cases legislators translate a bill's content into their own words. They apply their own terms or frames to simplify policies and turn them into actionable tidbits. Often this means relating the bill at hand to a previous experience, existing expertise, or other aspect of one's socialization.

If nothing else, members must be prepared to offer explanations for their behavior (Fenno 1978; Bianco 1994). Fenno highlighted the importance of explanations but did not probe into precisely how a member chooses among the many potential justifications available. It seems reasonable to assume that the explanations need to resonate with a member's reputation and be credible to interest groups, fellow members, and constituents. In many cases the resonance comes from a legislator's own knowledge and values. One personal experience or firsthand piece of expertise can dominate truckloads of technical reports, testimony, and lobbying. Specter's cancer scares provided him with a more vivid motivation than any information provided by the medical community. And Santorum's childbirth experience informed his views about partial birth abortion more effectively than did clergy, interest groups, or constituents.

Acknowledging these personal factors explains why Kingdon found that biased information is more desirable than objective information. It also fits with studies of decision making under limited information in the mass electorate. Popkin (1994), for example, offers Grisham's Law of Information, in which personal, recent, and vivid information tends to dominate impersonal, dated, and dry information. Even policymakers are susceptible to this heuristic if the personal information causes them to understand a piece of legislation differently than other factors in the field of forces do. Dry policy briefings have more resonance if they touch upon something that the legislator can understand easily in light of his own experiences. Having worked in the insurance industry or watched a family member deal with mental illness is the kind of experience that drives out impersonal information.

Readmitting this sort of complexity into congressional activity helps to better understand the "two Congresses" phenomenon, in which members seem to live different lives in their districts than they do in Washington. Without allowing for personal factors on the Hill, how can it be that Fenno's "home styles" are so idiosyncratic, personal, and varied, yet Washington behavior is so uniform, motivated as it is by a single political dimension? If the way a member cultivates his constituency is multidimensional, conditional, and personalized, then we must believe that his Washington style reflects some of these same tendencies. The winnowing that takes place during the legislative process does tend to simplify the dimensionality of legislation, often reducing the relevant considerations to just partisanship, ideology, and a couple of other factors (Jones, Talbert, and Potoski 2003; Talbert and Potoski 2002). But this does not necessarily mean that partisanship is all that concerns legislators, particularly when it comes to prefloor activities, where less packaging has been applied.

Appreciating the personal roots of representation helps one make better sense of the literature on legislative shirking. Most of the public choice literature on representation assumes that "legislators have policy preferences that differ from those of their constituents and that this difference can cause legislators to vote against the interest of their constituents, which are implicitly defined as the interests of the median voter in the political jurisdiction" (Bender and Lott 1996, 69). The main contributions to the literature on shirking take this perspective (Kalt and Zupan 1990; Kau and Rubin 1979; Peltzman 1984).[20] Uslaner (1999) points to the false dichotomy between constituency interests and personal ideology. In using a principal-agent framework, economists have typically viewed representation using an "either-or" model (Parker and Choi 2006): any legislator not perfectly fulfilling her constituents' wishes must be shirking, allowing her own worldview to affect her decisions. Yet real politics is messier than that.

Dichotomizing representation as just constituency versus personal ideology, or party versus preferences, presents a false choice. It requires an "either-or" result without acknowledging that these forces are seldom in real conflict. It also leaves out many other influences on legislators' behavior. Second, and more importantly, it fails to appreciate the full nature of political preferences. Arguing that a black box of preferences determines how a legislator behaves is only a bit better than tautology, because it stipulates that members do what they want to do. Normatively, it is crucial to know not only where a legislator stands but why.

Perhaps viewing ideology as the dominant factor in legislative decision-making is a reasonable way to explain roll call voting on a wide variety of issues. When many votes are scaled together, they tend to form a one- or two-dimensional space (Burden and Clausen 1998; Clinton, Jackman, and Rivers 2004; Poole and Rosenthal 1997). However consistent this finding, I believe that it does not necessarily generalize to individual policy domains or particular roll calls. On individual votes idiosyncratic factors become more important, and general patterns of behavior recede. It is the aggregation process used in creating voting indices that washes out most of the policy-specific factors that shape legislative outcomes. But it is individual votes on which legislators must bargain, form coalitions, and ultimately take action. I thus depart from the existing literature by approaching votes and narrow policy areas one at a time. It is in these cases that I expect the backgrounds of legislators to matter more that an aggregate analysis would reveal.

The few existing studies that happen to focus on a specific policy area support this view. Interviews with legislators find that personal interests in policy are strongly determined by occupational and personal experi-

[20] Note that a few authors expand the definition of shirking to include lack of effort (Bender and Lott 1996; Herrick, Moore, and Hibbing 1994; Parker 1992). Since I am examining policy responsiveness, I avoid this version of shirking.

ence, and to a lesser extent group identification (Gooch 2004). Especially in health care policy, personal experiences as consumers in the health care system provide a form of expertise. Female legislators are more likely to reflect on their own responsibilities for children and elderly parents, and the crises that accompany them, in deciding how to vote (Krajnak 2003). A study of the 1990 House vote on a constitutional amendment designed to ban flag burning is instructive (Lascher, Kelman, and Kane 1993). Basing their conclusions on a survey of representatives, the authors find that both legislators' personal views and their constituency influenced the vote. Abortion votes and other morality decisions in the House are strongly colored by representatives' religious affiliations (Oldmixon 2005; Page et al. 1984). Religious denominations are somewhat predictive of general ideological voting patterns, correlating with votes more strongly than do most district characteristics (Green and Guth 1991). Yet denominational affiliations have differential effects, depending on party affiliation. I shall return to these kinds of asymmetries below.

If members' interests are important, their influence should vary across issues. Even Heckman and Snyder (1997), who are frequently credited with validating the Poole-Rosenthal model of a unidimensional Congress, doubt that their aggregate estimates accurately reflect the dimensionality of the policy space. Trying to maximize the fit of roll call votes on a single dimension "may cause analysts to overlook preference factors that are tapped by relatively few roll calls," and these neglected factors "are critical for accurate prediction on certain specific issues" (1997, S174). Bianco concurs that "studies of the legislative process should aim at explaining individual decisions, such as a legislator's votes, rather than focusing on aggregates of individual-level decisions, such as ADA scores" (1994, 158). Indeed, Ansolabehere, Snyder, and Stewart (2001b) show that the relative weights of partisanship and ideology differ by policy area.

In the following two sections I briefly review two literatures that explode the existing paradigm further. First, I highlight recent work on legislative participation beyond roll call voting, or what I call proactive behavior. Although this research does a service in moving the analytical focus upstream in the policy process, it does not generally recognize the role of the legislator himself in determining when and where to be proactive. Second, I summarize several studies examining whether blacks and women legislative differently than white men. The findings in the literature are mixed. I suggest that my theoretical framework helps make sense of them by specifying the conditions under which personal characteristics like race and sex matter. In the end I argue that the lines of research on members' participation and members' characteristics should be combined rather than considered in isolation.

Research on Legislator Participation

In recent years a small number of political scientists has begun to examine behavior beyond roll call voting, focusing directly on participation in the legislative process. A pioneer in this subfield, Hall (1996) offers congressional scholars a new orientation by focusing on activity levels of members of Congress. His insights build on an earlier understanding that legislators must decide "not only how to vote but what to do with time, how to allocate resources, and where to put energy" (Bauer, Pool, and Dexter 1963, 405). Indeed, an older tradition in political science argued that "an adequate concept of representation should account for a total action pattern, not merely a final vote" (Jones 1961, 367). Fenno's (1986) close observations of legislators in action shows that intensity of views motivates involvement and attentiveness in actions other than the vote, which is a separate decision.

Among Hall's other contributions, he highlights the fact that participation is highly selective. Although legislators have to vote on all kinds of issues when they reach a floor vote, members choose a limited number on which to be active. Hall documents numerous committee and floor activities where only a small group of legislators are involved in more than a superficial way. Participation is heavily determined by expertise and interest, which in his view are often a product of subcommittee assignments and subconstituencies in the district. This is where I augment Hall's work by showing that these two factors are far from determinative. District interests and committee assignments do motivate members' behavior on most bills, but I propose that other individual-level traits are also part of the equation.

Taking a more abstract approach, Wawro (2001a) also finds great differences in participation rates across members. Perhaps because his focus is on "entrepreneurship" on the floor rather than in committee, he is unable to identify any correlates of participation. Only a desire to move up through the party hierarchy seems related to a member's entrepreneurship score. There are apparently no constituency, personal, or any other factors behind general activity levels, but that outcome may result from overlooking the content of legislation in creating the entrepreneurship score. Kessler and Krehbiel (1996), Koger (2003), Mayhew (2000), and Schiller (1995) likewise do not consider the content of sponsorship or other forms of participations but simply explain overall levels of activity. In Mayhew's (2000) treatment, personal motivations for proactivity are important but also seem too idiosyncratic to generalize. I expect that when activity on particular policies is studied instead, personal characteristics that bear on that policy will become salient.

If activity levels vary across members, the intensities of the preferences must vary as well. Deeply held axioms of formal theory have prevented most researchers (besides Hall) from comparing the intensities of legislators' preferences.[21] Yet any observer of the legislative process, or politics more generally, can see that some participants feel more intensely about an issue than do others. Their concern motivates action to amplify their otherwise minor role in the decision process. If roll call voting were all that legislators could do, on salient issues some representatives would like to vote many times to demonstrate their commitment! Since each member is given just one vote, the only way to register one's intensity is to become proactive in the prevote deliberations. Unable to vote multiple times, individuals try to influence the outcome by contributing time and effort to amplify their positions.

At the same time, others are so conflicted or uninterested that they hardly care to vote. Members of Congress do not usually have the luxury of abstention, however, since missing votes is bad electoral politics. The best these members can do is to *only* vote on the final bill, forgoing opportunities to comment, negotiate, amend, or lobby on behalf of the legislation earlier in the process. They might delay taking a position, hoping in fact that a floor vote will never happen, that the bill will be bottled up in committee or not scheduled for floor action (Kingdon 1989). But voting—as experts on citizen behavior such as Verba have noted—is the only form of influence that is distributed equally among all participants. Those who feel more strongly must resort to other means.

Time is perhaps a legislator's most valuable resource. Overscheduled and pulled in many ways by competing interests, a member must carefully allocate the hours available to him. As Fenno (1978) observed, representatives' two most important decisions are how to allocate time and, relatedly, staff. Information is also overly abundant. Legislators must find efficient ways to make sense of the information overload and must pick and choose issues on which to be active. Surely district interests play a role in both of these choices. When a dominant concern of one's constituents is invoked by a bill, a legislator will often seek additional information and become more involved. But on many issues that have little to do with the district, legislators resort to information shortcuts, often becoming active on matters where they happen to have some personal background. And personal factors can lead a legislator to become proactive on issues as well.

[21] This "cardinal" rule of social choice theory has deep origins but became more prominent when it became a critical part of Arrow's (1951) impossibility theorem. For critiques of this view see Elster and Roemer (1993).

Research on Race and Gender in Congress

Bucking the general tendency of political science to avoid considering the personal roots of legislators' behavior, recent research has examined the effects of race and sex extensively. A body of research emerged in the 1990s to evaluate whether female and black legislators behave differently than their male and white colleagues. Those studies were motivated by real-world developments, primarily the racial redistrictings following the 1990 census and the related "year of the woman" in 1992 that elected more women in Congress. Here I briefly review this literature, showing that its results, although seemingly inconsistent across studies, can be understood in light of my theory.

In one of the earliest studies of gender in the legislature, Thomas (1994) found that female state legislators were more likely to introduce legislation that dealt with women, children, and families but less likely to sponsor bills concerned with business. In a later study of women in Congress, Swers (2002) found that female representatives were more likely to sponsor legislation dealing with "women's issues." But it is noteworthy in Swers's evidence that the effect of gender on sponsorship varied by party: women were especially likely to support women's issue actively if they were Republican. "In fact," Swers concludes, "being a Republican woman exerted a more important influence on sponsorship of feminist legislation than any other variable including constituency characteristics, ideology, or committee position" (48). Republican women were also especially likely to introduce amendments to bills affecting women's issues, in committee and on the floor. A similar pattern emerged with regard to roll call votes, with Republican women and men diverging more than their Democratic counterparts.

Vega and Firestone (1995) found that gender did not have much impact on roll call votes through the 1980s, but began to have a modest impact in the 1990s. (Ethnicity has always had a substantial influence.) While sex did not affect voting patterns much, Vega and Firestone's evidence suggests two other intriguing results. First, women, particularly Democratic women, voted more cohesively than did other groups. Second, sex affected the introduction of "women's issues" bills much more than it did roll call votes.

Evans (2005) shows that sex does not affect the overall ideological voting patterns of Democratic representatives, but among Republicans women do vote differently than men. This finding mirrors Swers's result about the asymmetric role played by gender within the two parties. Beyond her interest in gender effects, Evans shows that except for district ideology, none of the variables behaves the same in the Democratic and Republican models. But Evans goes further than Swers, demonstrating that sex behaves differently in explaining party unity voting. It affects members of both parties equally, but in opposite directions. Women are about six points more partisan in the Democratic caucus but six points less partisan as Republicans.

As for studies of race, an early salvo from Swain (1993) argues that black and white legislators are able to represent black constituents equally well. Assuming a tension between descriptive and substantive representation, Swain laments that black constituents tend to favor the former over the latter. But she finds that (Democratic) representatives who happen to be white can advocate for the policy wishes of black constituents as well as African-American legislators do. Although Swain does not estimate a fully specified regression model, the qualitative evidence suggests that a legislator's race is unrelated to his or her roll call voting patterns. Canon (1999) expands this line of thinking, suggesting that positions of black and white incumbents are quite similar. Importantly, however, black legislators often do a better job of representing both black and white constituent interests.

But this finding has been disputed. Cameron, Epstein, and O'Halloran (1996) argue, in direct contrast to Swain, that black representatives in fact vote differently on civil rights bills than do white Democrats. Despite disagreeing with arguments about the merits of racial redistricting, Lublin (1997) agrees that black representatives are somewhat more responsive to black constituents than are white Democrats, although the difference is much smaller than the difference between Democratic and Republican representatives.

In an attempt to separate different sorts of roll call votes, Whitby (1997) finds that black representatives vote differently than white representatives on amendments but not generally on final passage of legislation. In addition to showing variability in these effects from one congress to the next, race seems to matter more "upstream" during the amending process than "downstream" at the final roll call.

Although the study of women and blacks (and implicitly men and whites) has dominated the literature, occasionally other demographic groups are studied. Haider-Markel, Joslyn, and Kniss (2000) find that openly gay officeholders are more likely to support domestic partner benefits. Yet much like Swain's result, heterosexual representatives who have supportive values can also represent gays and lesbians adequately. Bianco (2005) finds that the massive decline in the number of veterans in the House does not have much effect on key defense and foreign policy votes. Apparently veterans' and nonveterans' descriptive differences do not translate into substantive outcomes. Miller (1995) argues that the dominance of lawyers in Congress leads a focus on rights and procedures. Finally, Washington

(2005) shows that male representatives with daughters are significantly more likely to cast liberal roll call votes on women's issues, particularly those related to abortion.

Beyond roll call voting, one study suggests that women and blacks are more likely to sponsor legislation that deals with women's and blacks' interests (Bratton and Haynie 1999). But these are ambiguous results because the models do not control for underlying tendencies to sponsor bills. The data show that women are also more likely to sponsor legislation related to black interests, and blacks to sponsor legislation related to women's interest. We do not know if this result is genuine cross-endorsement of the other group's interests or a general tendency of underrepresented groups to sponsor legislation of all kinds. The authors do not examine sponsorship of other kinds of legislation. Moreover, studies of congressional sponsorship activity fail to control for sex and race (Koger 2003; Schiller 1995). Whether blacks and women—or any other group—tend to be more active on particular kinds of legislation remains an unanswered question.

Beyond the potential for descriptive representation to shape policy outcomes, there may be other normative reasons for supporting it. Mansbridge (1999) argues that the benefits of descriptive representation (such as greater faith in government and more innovation) often outweigh the costs (such as less expertise). Descriptive representation may also bond constituents to their government, thereby raising levels of knowledge and trust (Banducci, Donovan, and Karp 2004; Burns, Schlozman, and Verba 2001; Gay 2002; Mansbridge 1999; Tate 2001). Being represented by someone with different racial or other characteristics can also discourage political engagement (Banducci, Donovan, and Karp 2004; Gay 2001).

But Mansbridge believes that descriptive representation also yields policy benefits for underrepresented groups. In Mansbridge's framework, whether it is worth having a woman represent women and a black represent blacks is contingent. It depends on how novel an issue is and whether the parties have developed clear positions. Extending Mansbridge's argument, my theory helps specify the conditions under which descriptive characteristics are important. It also alerts researchers to other characteristics beyond race and sex, which are perhaps the most obvious of physical traits. And it pushes the analysis upstream in the legislative process, where personal characteristics are more likely to be influential.

Because most research focuses solely on roll call voting, we do not know much about how the variables thought to influence legislators operate at different stages of the legislative process. Although necessary for the passage of legislation, roll call votes represent an unusual point in the process. As others have noted (Cox and McCubbins 2005; Van Doren 1990), votes are the most passive of activities, and their outcomes are often predetermined by party leaders who control the legislative agenda. As a result, they display an inordinate amount of partisanship and ideology. But the dominance of partisanship gives way to a more variegated set of influences as we begin to step back from the current scholarly paradigm. Disaggregating voting scales to analyze roll calls individually is likely to show less partisanship and more autonomy for the representative. I hypothesize that, as one moves upstream in the legislative process, partisanship and ideology recede in their dominance, making room for personal factors to become operable. In the days before a vote comes to the floor, members must be proactive if they wish to play a part in the deliberations. They face opportunities to give floor speeches, cosponsor amendments, and lobby fellow members. But each of these tasks takes precious time and is not undertaken lightly. A legislator must have good reasons to take on these selective activities. I expect that background characteristics, which serve as proxies for interests, values, and expertise, are more consequential than party membership and ideology in explaining these early proactive behaviors.

Moreover, the effects are often asymmetric. Legislators who feel threatened by change in the status quo are most likely to mobilize their interests. Typically in the minority, these representatives who see their interests and values being challenged are especially likely to become active on an issue. In contrast, for those supporting the proposed policy changes, more standard variables such as ideology and district preferences remain important. As a result, background variables are better predictors of legislative behavior on one side of the issue than the other. Although this asymmetry will not appear on every issue, it has the potential to distort the representative process. Legislators become the most susceptible to internal cues precisely at points in the policymaking process in which their influence is greatest and their divergence from constituents' preferences may be as well. Unless voters have selected representatives on the basis of personal characteristics, legislative behavior can deviate a great deal from the pluralistic and median voter models thought to characterize delegate-style representation. Where a legislator stands is only of modest importance. Knowing why she stands where she does and what the consequences of her positions are is far more critical.

To evaluate these claims, my empirical approach in the following chapters is to make direct comparisons between reactive roll call voting and proactive speechmaking and bill cosponsorship. I also examine floor rhetoric to reveal the personal justifications that members give for their actions. When analyzing speeches and cosponsorship, I disaggregate the results according to which side of an issue a legislator is on, to reveal asymmetries in the effects of background variables on action. Although the data are sometimes limiting, I carry this approach through case studies of policymaking in the areas of tobacco regulation, education, and religion and morality. In each setting I limit the scope to a single policy area and often to individual bills. In all three cases I find that legislators' personal traits become more important as one moves upstream in the policy process and generally as one shifts from opponents to proponents of the status quo.

Conclusion

This chapter advocates a new orientation to the study of congressional behavior. I began by acknowledging that congressional action is driven by many factors. Among them are constituency preferences, ideology, and partisanship. Indeed, the control that party leaders hold over the legislative agenda often means that roll call votes have a heavily partisan or ideological character. As well as these variables explain the aggregate voting patterns of legislators, they do not explain them all. They are even less potent in explaining votes on specific legislation and proactive behavior such as making speeches and sponsoring bills, precisely the situations where legislators' actions are more consequential in shaping policy outcomes. My theory expects that in these situations personal characteristics will be meaningful influences on legislative action. The greater importance of legislators themselves in such cases often outweighs other factors such as constituents' preferences. Ironically, this inhibits members' responsiveness at just the places in the policy process where voters' views could have the most influence on outcomes. In earlier stages of the policymaking process there are fewer participants, whose actions reverberate downstream until the bill expires or a roll call vote is taken.

In addition to stressing upstream activity and personal characteristics, my theory highlights the asymmetric effects of variables. Personal traits and other variables are often important only for those on one side of the debate. In particular, I suggest that backgrounds tend to be more determinative for the minority coalition and for those opposing change in the status quo. Although this asymmetry is not likely to hold in every case, it highlights the fact that responsiveness to constituents' wishes varies from member to member, depending on personal motivations and other factors.

CHAPTER THREE

Smoking and Tobacco Regulation

CONGRESS IN THE 1990S BEGAN WRESTLING more vigorously than it had in a long time with tobacco. The legislature considered a range of significant changes including new restrictions on tobacco advertising, increased taxes on tobacco products, and revised standards for tobacco company liability. Each member of Congress had to come to terms with these new policy choices, providing answers to two questions: "What position do I take?" and "How active should I be in furthering these positions?" This chapter takes a look at the responses to these questions on tobacco policy in the 104th House of Representatives. In the midst of the tobacco wars of the 1990s, these were no minor decisions.

The chapter covers a great deal of empirical ground. The first half provides a foundation for studying where members stood on tobacco policy by providing some historical context for the issues involved. I note that the status quo of existing tobacco subsidies and lighter regulations was threatened in the 1990s. As a consequence, those opposed to further tobacco regulation were on the defensive. Smoking rates were also on the decline, and the Clinton administration openly advocated stricter control of tobacco. After documenting some of these dynamics, I then to turn to issues of representation by describing how tobacco use in the population compares with tobacco use in Congress. Smokers are underrepresented in Washington, which means that many constituents who use tobacco are represented by House members who do not. This discord provides an opportunity for personal factors to influence legislative behavior in way that many constituents would oppose.

The second half of the chapter analyzes how members act on tobacco policy. I begin by examining rhetoric on the House floor to demonstrate how members frame issues by translating them into personalized, simplified terms. I then explain members' floor votes, the quintessential reactive form of legislative activity. Where members stand on roll calls is determined by their public ideologies and the economic interests of their district, with other variables playing only supporting roles. But new variables become important when the dependent variable is replaced with a proactive measure such as speechmaking or cosponsoring a bill. Examining these more active legislative behaviors reveals asymmetries between those with opposing positions. As expected, the effects are conditional on partisanship and on which side of the issue a member is located. In particular, the interests of legislators and their constituents become more important among those most threatened by proposed changes to the status quo. Finally, an analysis of contributions from tobacco PACs reveals that donors are aware of this pattern and give disproportionately to legislators with a personal interest and those who are active on the issue.

The Political Importance of Tobacco

Tobacco policy makes an intriguing case study for a number of theoretical and empirical reasons. First, tobacco issues have been visible on the national political agenda, particularly in the late 1990s. The scope of tobacco's reach in American politics is difficult to overstate. The expanding debate over tobacco policy in America managed to find its way into each branch of the federal government. It has been on the agenda in most if not all of the states and has energized interest groups, the media, and other extragovernmental actors on all sides of the issue (Baumgartner and Jones 1993; Derthick 2001).

Second, tobacco policy is multifaceted. It is both an economic and a noneconomic policy issue since it touches upon morality and public health concerns. While the economics of the tobacco industry—taxes, jobs, and trade—are often salient, the rights of smokers and nonsmokers are also at stake. A limitation of a purely economic study is that one must assume that all actors have insatiable appetites for income or benefits, thus inducing a sort of artificial homogeneity of preferences. In contrast, tobacco preferences are far from uniform. The smoking cleavage divides people into two rough camps with different interests and different stakes in the game. Some representatives will have an intimate knowledge of the tobacco industry from working in it or with it. Others will have a direct sense of the good and bad economic consequences of tobacco farming. Yet others, with or without this experience, will focus on either public health concerns that favor tobacco restrictions or civil liberties criteria that favor government restraint. This diversity of interests allows for richer analyses of their effects.

Third, tobacco policies on cigarette taxation and where a person may smoke in public are remarkably unambiguous and salient (Green and Gerken 1989). Unlike some more distant issues such as foreign trade and mining on federal lands, smoking regulations have clear personal effects and thus hit home more directly. The personal component of tobacco makes it an ideal target for probing the effects of self-interest. The ability to "light up" without restriction is a symbolic reminder about personal liberty in American society, much the way riding a motorcycle without a helmet is. And the policies (aside from, perhaps, the level of subsidies for tobacco farmers and tobacco companies) have quite visible manifestations. Paying more for cigarettes, seeing advertising at a sporting event or in a magazine, and sitting in a smoke-free restaurant are immediate and personal consequences of the policymaking process.

The Clinton years are a particularly interesting time to put tobacco policymaking under the microscope. Until the late 1990s federal action on tobacco took place outside of Congress, coming in the form of studies and recommendations from the Surgeon General and others. Aside from requiring health warnings on cigarette packs and limiting tobacco advertising in the 1960s and occasional (and often temporary) changes in subsidies and taxes thereafter, Congress had done relatively little in the area. Changes, modest as they were, occurred primarily in the courts and via regulatory agencies such as the Food and Drug Administration (cf. Derthick 2001).[1] Antitobacco (or procontrol) action from the Clinton administration (and Clinton's FDA administrator, David Kessler) in the nineties was thus something of a change in the environment, coming as it did in the wake of revelations from tobacco companies about their practices over the past few decades (Studlar 2002).[2]

Moreover, as figures 3.1 and 3.2 demonstrate, smokers became a smaller and more stigmatized minority over time. Beyond being pushed outside of restaurants, offices, and other public areas, tobacco users became fewer in number. Figure 3.1 shows that, beginning in the mid-1970s, tobacco consumption (here measured as cigarette sales per capita) fell quite dramatically. Consumption was cut roughly in half between 1980 and 2000. There are two sources for this reduction. Part of the decline stems from smokers who began smoking less, either for health reasons or because smoking became more inconvenient.

The bigger reason for declining consumption is that there were fewer smokers in the population. Figure 3.2 shows that the percentage of American adults calling themselves smokers fell from more than 40% in 1965 to around 23% in 2000.[3] In less than 40 years smokers went from being nearly half of the adult population to less than a quarter. An interesting aspect of this reduction is that it occurs more dramatically among men. As male smoking rates were cut by half, the gender gap in smoking shrank

[1] See the tobacco history timeline at <http://www.tobacco.org>.

[2] In the remainder of this chapter I refer to the two camps as those "for" and those "against" further tobacco regulation. This is an attempt to avoid the confusing labeling of a person as "pro" or "anti" tobacco.

[3] The technical definition of a "current smoker" is one who reports smoking at least 100 cigarettes a year and smoke every day (until 1992) or at least some days each week (1992 onward).

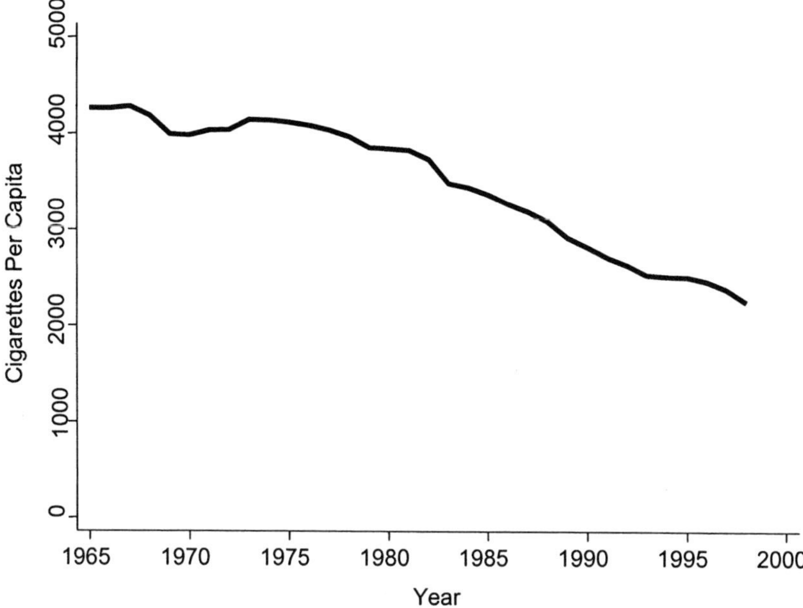

Figure 3.1. Cigarette consumption per capita (1965–98). *Note:* Cigarette consumption per American adult taken from U.S. Department of Agriculture.

tremendously. The difference in men's and women's tobacco use rates decreased from roughly 16 percentage points to less than five points. Smoking is thus significantly less common and less gendered than it was a generation ago.

These changes in the prevalence and overall consumption of tobacco products in the United States put antiregulation forces on the defensive during the "tobacco wars" of the 1990s. Those in the tobacco industry—farmers, distributors, and marketers—felt persecuted. Smokers, even those who wanted to quit, often felt stigmatized and challenged. In short, the threat to friends of tobacco was near an all time high.

If the theoretical framework outlined in the first two chapters is accurate, one ought to observe asymmetries between those for and those against greater tobacco control. Although the latter might attempt simply to resist as the proregulation forces approached, the former smelled blood in the water and had public opinion on their side. Public and symbolic behaviors, such as floor speeches, ought to be more strongly connected to personal factors among those supporting tighter restrictions. In contrast, more substantive proactive behaviors, such as introduction and sponsorship of bills, should be related to tobacco use by those defending the

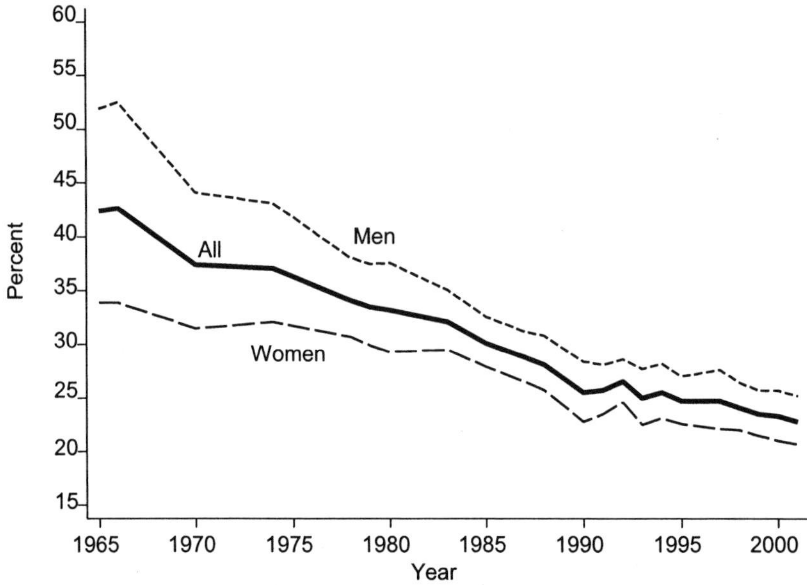

Figure 3.2. Smoking prevalence among U.S. adults (1965–2001). *Note:* Estimates of percentage of adult population who are current smokers taken from Centers for Disease Control. A slight aberration in the data occurs in 1992 because of a redefinition of "current" smoker.

status quo. To complicate matters further, these differences ought to be conditional on party affiliation since it was primarily the Democrats who were advocating change. The tobacco wars of the 1990s were notable because they were frequently, though not entirely, fought along party lines. It was a Democratic President Clinton, after all, who became the aggressor in these events, while Republicans were more likely to defend smokers and the tobacco industry.

Tobacco and Representation

Because tobacco use has political ramifications for average Americans, one might suspect that the same applies to policymakers. Legislators who smoke probably differ from their nonsmoking colleagues in some important ways. In the midst of the tobacco wars, smokers were likely to feel threatened or at least more heavily scrutinized than in the past. According to my account, there should be asymmetries in the kinds of proactive and reactive behaviors engaged in by tobacco users and nonusers. Before exploring these relationships, the data I will use require some description.

Measures of representatives' tobacco use are taken from an unconventional source. In 1997 *Roll Call Online,* an Internet version of the Beltway publication *Roll Call,* compiled a list of tobacco users serving in the 104th Congress.[4] All were cigarette or cigar smokers, so it parallels the constituent measure that also relies on reported use of smoked tobacco products. The list revealed that smokers make up about 7% of members (30 in the House and six in the Senate).[5] Around the same time, the 1996 American National Election Study (NES) asked, for the first time, about tobacco use. In response to a direct question, "Are you a smoker?" 24% of NES respondents reported yes. This is quite close to the CDC estimates highlighted earlier. Because both datasets are national in scope and cover the same time period, I merge them to create a hybrid dataset containing information on both constituents and representatives. By matching constituents to their particular legislators, dyadic analyses may be conducted as well.

I suspect that both measures underestimate tobacco usage. The NES probably depresses smoking figures slightly because some smokers report inaccurately, either out of social desirability or their own intentions to quit. The congressional list may not have detected some covert tobacco users on Capitol Hill.[6] Yet it is well known that elected officials are often drawn from the activist pool and tend to have higher incomes, more education, and generally greater resources than the average citizen (Verba, Schlozman, and Brady 1995). Given the socioeconomic differences between smokers and nonsmokers, it is not surprising that members of Congress are much less likely to use tobacco than the public at large. Although 7% of Congress as smokers seems low, the figure is quite similar to the rate in the general population once the NES sample is restricted to those who are demographically similar to members of Congress. For example, members of the House are far more educated than the general public: near all are college graduates and most have advanced degrees (Amer 1999). Among college graduates in the NES only 13% smoke; among those with advanced degrees only 8.5% smoke. This suggests that members of the House are not out of step with their demographic peers.

Given the tendency of Democrats to smoke more than Republicans in

[4] "The Smokers' Caucus" was accessed at <http://www.rollcall.com/rcfiles/smokerslist.html> in September 1997.

[5] Another 2% were "recent quitters."

[6] Although *Roll Call* did not list him as a smoker, Trent Lott (R-MS) admitted on *Meet the Press* in July 2000 that he occasionally smokes a pipe. Either Lott picked up the habit in the three years since the list was published or he was mistakenly excluded.

the electorate, it is surprising that Republican members of the House are slightly more likely than the Democrats to smoke. This makes the smokers a more conservative group. Using Poole and Rosenthal's (1997) W-NOMINATE measure as a general indicator of ideological positions, the average smoker in the House (.311) is substantially to the right of the typical nonsmoking member (.150).[7] Citizens who smoke are more liberal than nonsmokers at all socioeconomic levels; why the relationships between ideology, party, and tobacco use are reversed at the elite level of Congress is unclear.

The underrepresentation of smokers in Congress will only have meaningful policy consequences if tobacco use relates to politically relevant variables such as attitudes toward tobacco regulation. I explore this possibility beginning with the classic distinction between *collective* and *dyadic* representation. Collective representation assesses how an elected body resembles the aggregate electorate, while dyadic representation occurs in representative-district pairs (Hill and Hurley 1999; Miller and Stokes 1963; Weissberg 1978). A constituent's characteristics may be represented either by her own representative or collectively by representatives from other districts. For example, although many African-Americans are not represented by black members of Congress, the overall representation of blacks in the House is close to that in the public (roughly 10% in the House and 13% in the electorate). Although these two forms of representation are not equivalent, both are *descriptive* representation, in Pitkin's (1967) framework, and I assume that either kind will be consequential because of its implications for *substantive* representation. That is, legislators and constituents are compared with respect to the distribution of a characteristic among them under the assumption, which I later test, that such characteristics lead to different policy choices.

The results of a simple legislator-constituent cross-tabulation are presented in table 3.1. Collectively, smokers were underrepresented in the 104th Congress. Recall that only about 6% of House districts (30 out of 435) were represented by smokers despite the fact that one in four Americans used tobacco.[8] This difference leaves a 20 percentage point gap in collective representation, that is, the underrepresentation of smokers. Perhaps many smokers are concentrated in regions of country also repre-

[7] As noted in chapter 1, first dimension NOMINATE scores use roll call votes to scale legislators on a continuum from −1 (most liberal) to +1 (most conservative). The mean W-NOMINATE score in the 104th House was .169.

[8] The percentage of representatives who smoke is reported at 5.5% rather than 6% in the table because the NES tends to oversample districts with nonsmoking legislators slightly. The NES sampling frame provides a reasonable sample of respondents but not necessarily a representative collection of districts.

TABLE 3.1
Collective and Dyadic Representation of Smokers

		Constituent Smokes?		
		No	*Yes*	*Total*
Representative Smokes?	No	72% (1,098)	23% (346)	95% 1,444
	Yes	4% (68)	1% (15)	5% (83)
	Total	76% (1,166)	24% (361)	

Note: Constituent data from 1996 NES. House data from *Roll Call.*

sented by tobacco users. It is telling that the gap is larger for the representation of women (35 points), who are geographically dispersed, but much smaller for blacks (three points), who are geographically concentrated. Descriptive representation depends in part on how widely distributed the trait is across constituencies, as I explain further in the book's concluding chapter. The fact that the NES survey draws a representative sample of American adults allows us to match representatives and constituents based on the congressional districts in which respondents live.

Nearly all nonsmoking constituents are represented by nonsmokers, but there are many smokers—nearly a quarter of the entire populance—who are represented by nonsmokers. The wide dispersal of smokers around the country coupled with the collective representation gap guarantees that dyadic representation will be less than perfect. In fact, the relationship between constituent and representative tobacco use is insignificant ($\chi^2 = 1.51, p = .22$). This is ironic since smoking at the citizen level has a Democratic bias while smoking in Congress has a Republican bias, and Republicans held a 30-seat majority in the 104th House. Normatively, one might be encouraged by this table, as 73% of constituents are in "congruent" cells. However, almost all of the concordant pairs are nonsmokers represented by nonsmokers.

Most important for our purposes are the many instances in which tobacco use patterns of constituents and their representatives differ. It is these cases in which legislators' personal views conflict with other forces and it becomes possible to separate their effects. A legislator who smokes cigarettes regularly will face tobacco issues in Congress on which he is required to take a position, knowing that most of his constituents are nonsmokers. In these cases it is important to determine whether constituents' preferences, interest group lobbying, ideology, or pure self-interest will dominate.

Positioning on Tobacco Policy

My argument posits that under particular conditions, members' interests, values, and experiences are significant forces that shape their policy actions. Here I rely on a measure of tobacco use as a proxy for one of these personal factors. All else equal, one should expect smoking representatives to be more protobacco than their nonsmoking colleagues. I tackle roll call voting first, where asymmetries between smokers and nonsmokers ought to be least consequential.

Some crude evidence for a personal motive in voting on tobacco legislation may be found by simply comparing smoking and nonsmoking legislators' voting records. To summarize legislators' positions on tobacco legislation, I use rating from SmokeFree Action, an antitobacco interest group. Like other interest groups that rate members' roll call voting records, SmokeFree Action computes the percentage of time each legislator took positions that favored tobacco regulation, ranging from 0 to 100.[9] A protobacco position opposes restrictions on tobacco advertising and constraints on where individuals may smoke while protecting the tobacco industry from regulation and litigation.

Figure 3.3 shows the distributions of smoking and nonsmoking members of Congress on the SmokeFree Action score. The average nonsmoker in the House had a mean SmokeFree Action score of 43.5, while the mean smoking legislator was at 25.1, a difference of more than 18 points. While nonsmokers show a real diversity of positions by being distributed somewhat evenly over the interval, smokers are decidedly to the left (de Guia et al. 2003). The clumping of smokers on the low end of scale points to the expected asymmetry of interests where those in the minority are more homogeneous and connected by a common interest.

My model reminds us that simple differences between smokers and nonsmokers cannot be immediately attributed to personal factors. Legislative behavior is the result the entire "field of forces" acting on a legislator. These forces include internal factors such as values and expertise but also external cues taken from parties, and information provided by

[9] According to the group's own definition, "Smokefree Action was founded by veteran anti-tobacco health advocates from across the United States to address forthrightly key issues relating to the politics of tobacco." Unlike other interest group ratings, the SmokeFree Action score includes some items that are not roll call votes. In addition to the five roll calls dealing with tobacco regulation, law suits, and subsidies are indicators of whether members signed anti- or pro-FDA regulation letters. Legislators are not penalized for missing votes.

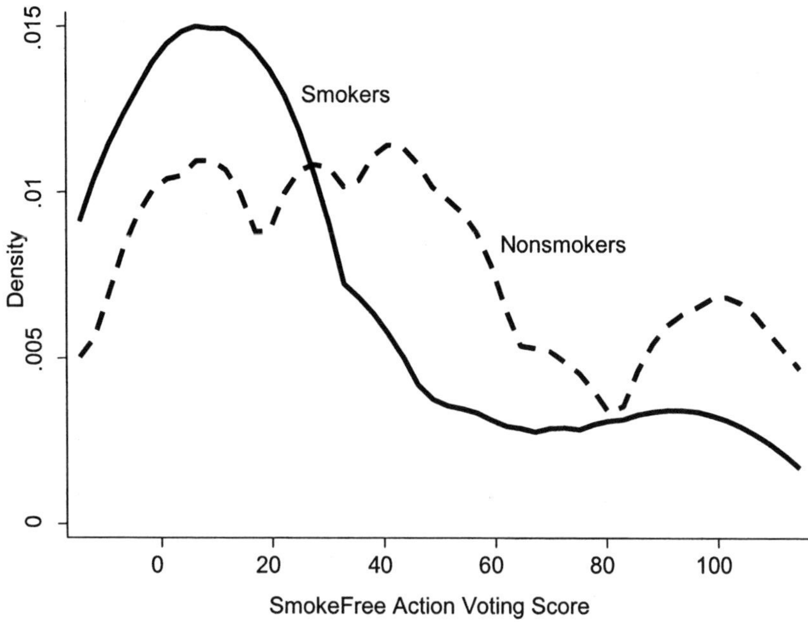

Figure 3.3. SmokeFree Action scores of smokers and nonsmokers (104th House)

interest groups. A multivariate model of legislators' actions on tobacco is needed to test simultaneously the hypotheses found in figure 2.1.

Before moving to data analysis, it is appropriate to explore the plausibility of personal factors as motivations by exploring how members justify their positions in their own words. Votes—just like bill introductions and cosponsorships—are rather crude indicators of why legislators do what they do. Roll call votes do not allow legislators to justify their positions. Explanations, Fenno tells us, are as important as the votes themselves. Explanations are remarkably consistent across venues, so we might expect floor rhetoric to be reasonably representative of members' explanations more generally. On the other hand, a sophisticated observer will not necessarily take the reasons given in floor speeches at face value (Hill and Hurley 2002). For example, a member might justify his opposition to new cigarette taxes with a free speech rationale yet also oppose it because he does not want to pay more for cigarettes himself. With this possibility in mind, it is nonetheless instructive to identify the frames used by members in their support or opposition to new tobacco control measures. It would be foolish to jump to the conclusion that the rationales provided in floor speeches actually explain voting patterns. I have already argued that the former is proactive while the latter is reactive, so they should respond to somewhat different stimuli. Yet a cursory look at floor rhetoric provides some insight into how members' rationalize their positions in their own words.

Congressional Rhetoric

The tobacco wars of the 1990s fascinated observers in part because of the motley mix of values and interests that they invoked. Tobacco issues put the free marketplace up against big government regulation, populist control over social behavior against individual liberty, corporation influence in Washington versus autonomy of the family farmer, and was just part of the new intersection of public health, budgetary mandates, and medicine (Derthick 2001). Any number of frames might be used to defend one's position on tobacco. A representative could argue that nicotine is a drug worthy of greater regulation. Another might oppose regulations on the grounds that they hurt small businesses and devalue hard work and family farms. Others might view tobacco companies as special interests whose influence should be curtailed. More libertarian members could view tobacco use as a freedom that ought to be protected from government encroachment. It is with this constitutional view that we begin.

I examine floor statements from the *Congressional Record* during the 104th House, the same Congress for which I have SmokeFree Action scores and NES data. I conducted a comprehensive search of the *Record,* identifying every instance in which a member mentioned tobacco policy on the House floor. Although I omit some of these statements because of their repetitiveness or tangential connection to tobacco, the following analysis provides a fair sampling of what members had to say about tobacco in the 104th House.

Some members defined the issue strictly in terms of civil liberties. At least for adults, the argument goes, government ought not limit behavior without strong reason. Even unpopular actions ought to be protected so that liberty more generally may be preserved. Take the following statement on the House floor by Walter Jones (R-NC).

> Most of us from North Carolina feel very strongly that youth, people 18 years and younger, should not be smoking cigarettes, and there is a State law that prevents that from happening. But we do feel adults, those 18 years and older, it is their constitutional right to make a decision whether they want to smoke or not. I do not smoke cigarettes. I do not have any tobacco allotments. But my wife does smoke, and that is her privilege. (July 24, 1995, H7545)

Interestingly, this same argument has been used by some politicians who straddle the abortion divide. I am personally opposed to abortion, one might say, and would neither abort a fetus nor condone such action by a family member. But I would hesitate to render abortion illegal nationwide for those of majority age. That is imposing one's values on a society. Here Representative Jones has an analogous argument for tobacco. He does not smoke, implies that tobacco use is not positive or productive, yet would never want to implement tobacco restrictions on adults.

In a legislative environment, the terms of debate are not the same as when one citizen discusses an issue with another. Disagreements in the workplace or family are merely opinions bumping into one another, with no real action to be taken. If opinions differ, the discussants must simply agree to disagree. But in the legislature action is to be taken. It is this end game to which many legislators' statements ultimately point. In winding down his floor statement, Representative Thomas Ewing (R-IL) made an appeal to parliamentary procedure rather than the substantive debate itself.

> But the issue of smoking, not one person has gotten up and said, "I like to smoke." I am not going to, either. I am a reformed smoker. I do not think we should smoke. My children do not smoke. I did not want them to smoke. But the point is, if you want to legislate on that issue, the appropriation process is not the place for the debate and not the place to decide that. We should do that in the substantive committee. That is where it ought to go. (June 12, 1996, H6226)

This move attempts to separate current congressional action from any general legislative statement about tobacco use restrictions. Perhaps Ewing feared the House would vote for tobacco control at the time, and not wanting to rile the opposition, tried to steer the debate to colder and more distant procedural territory. We cannot know for sure whether Ewing is a sincere parliamentarian here, holding principled views about separating substantive policy decisions from an appropriations bill, or whether this is merely cover for an ambiguous position that might displease constituents, colleagues, and interest groups should it be fully revealed.

Republicans opposed to tobacco control were quite willing to delegate the task of fighting the bill to members who could provide an economic defense. The GOP is typically viewed as stronger than the Democrats on fiscal issues (Petrocik 1996); this angle of attack uses those advantages to take a position that might be indefensible on public health grounds. Much like the debate about protection of endangered species versus logging jobs in the Pacific Northwest, these arguments focused on the detrimental economic impacts of new regulations and taxes. Members who could testify on behalf of the small tobacco farmer were privileged. Sometimes the party was looking for a credible spokesperson. Other times the member acted on her own initiative.

Republican Jones of North Carolina speaks again. "In my district alone . . . there are 11,500 tobacco farms." These farmers are not the enemy, he contends, but are in fact contributors to the common good. "The small tobacco farmer also contributes more than $30 million annually in various assessments" (H7545). Knowing that Jones represents a district dependent on tobacco crop production, these words do not sound terribly different from Mayhewian position taking. Rather than discuss broad principles, the congressman is merely defending his district from an adverse action by the legislature.

Another approach suggests that the proregulation camp is using the wrong tactics to limit tobacco use. A bill aimed at a few large tobacco companies might actually harm small business people. Consider the following statements pointing to the detrimental impacts on local farmers.

> I understand that there are many Members in this House who would like to make a political statement against smoking. But this is surely not the right way to go about it. This amendment will do nothing to stop smoking, but it will cause a lot of harm to tobacco farmers and the farming communities that depend on them. Many of these communities are located in my district. (Norman Sisisky D-VA, June 12, 1996, H6220)

> Most importantly I believe this amendment is aimed at the cigarette industry. However, the victim will not be the industry, it will be the small tobacco farmer. In my State of North Carolina the production of tobacco employs approximately 260,000 people. More specifically, 1 in 12 people have a tobacco-related job. A "yes" vote will be a vote to destroy the North Carolina economy. (Walter Jones R-NC, June 12, 1996, H6220)

Most members from districts like these are aware of the plight of small tobacco farmers from working the district, but this is often secondhand experience. A few members can actually provide testimony from firsthand experience. Scotty Baesler (D-KY) begins his floor statement by identifying himself this way. "Mr. Chairman, I probably have a little more unique position or consideration of this amendment than most Members because I am the only tobacco farmer in this House" (H6223). These personal experiences help convey the tough economic and emotional realities of the tobacco farm life. Another personal account:

> I had the good fortune to marry a young lady who grew up on a tobacco farm, and we spent hours and hours talking about what it was like growing up on that tobacco farm when her father would have to go and mortgage the land to plant his crop and how when the crop came in and after they got through curing it and they got through selling it, how he would go back to the bank, if they had a good year, and pay off the mortgage. And she talked about how many years they would have to go back and renew that mortgage and hope that they could make a better crop the next year, and in the meantime the land did not

get foreclosed on. Her father always said, "I hope that life for our children won't be as bad on this tobacco farm as it has been for me." (Sanford Bishop D-GA, June 12, 1996, H6225)

Surprisingly, race enters the dialogue here. But it is not playing the "race card" of the plight of blacks in the American South. Rather, tobacco farming is viewed as venue for pursing the American Dream, as a means of overcoming the constraints of race. Hard work is rewarded, regardless of race. No industry that does so much for lessening racial inequalities should be squelched with taxes or other regulations. Another African-American legislator explains.

> Mr. Chairman, I remember when my father used to pull tobacco over there in Quincy in Monticello, FL. That is the only place my daddy could get a job. I am from Tallahassee, FL. During those days, black Americans could not get a job in north Florida doing anything, but he was able to go on to this farmer industry and get a job. They did not ask him if he came from Carroll's Quarters. They did not ask him anything. I will never forget that. These small farmers, I think many of us do not understand what it means to be economically viable by using the farm. And this country was built on the farming industry. It helps to keep us all going. I will vote against anything. If Members go against peanuts, I will vote against them there. If Members go against tobacco, I will vote against them there. (Carrie Meek D-FL, June 12, 1996, H6231)

The framing here is not about tobacco per se; the specific crop is irrelevant in Meek's account. The point is that the opportunities provided by tobacco make an apparently immoral industry moral. Tobacco provides opportunity, particularly for minorities looking for an honest day's work. This might be a difficult story to spin for the public generally, but it did not stop members of the House from trying, as a member from Kentucky pleaded.

> I grew up on a hillside farm. We grew rocks on a very small farm. We also have a small patch of tobacco, and that was the only way that my father could raise this family, and send us to school, and buy the food on which we lived. That story is repeated 100,000 times around this country every year. We are not Philip Morris. We are not big tobacco. We are little. And we are poor. And we are scrapping, just trying to earn a living on 2 acres or 1 acre of tobacco. (Harold Rogers R-KY, June 12, 1996, H6234)

It was not uncommon for those defending the status quo to use multiple justifications. In a classic "kitchen sink" approach, Walter Jones added the local economic impact theme to the appeals to liberty and the American Dream, hoping that at least one of the reasons for defending the status quo would stick. In his ideological worldview, government regulation hurts people more than it helps, but this libertarian take is all the more true in the tobacco realm. "So if you look at what the FDA Director, Dr. Kessler . . . wants to classify nicotine as a drug . . . when I share those numbers with the people that are employed and what it means in salaries and revenue . . ." Kessler's plan would have clear negative consequences (Walter Jones R-NC, July 24, 1995, H7545).

Unlike those opposing tobacco regulation, members pushing for further FDA restrictions and higher taxes tended to focus on just one or two arguments. In contrast to Representative Jones's tactics of offering many arguments for his position, most of the proregulation camp focused solely on public health. Nearly every member wishing to change the status quo said in one way or another that tobacco is addictive and seriously harmful. Tobacco production, distribution, advertisement, and use should be severely restricted to protect the public's health.

The only exception was Marty Meehan (D-MA), who had hitched his fortunes to the campaign finance star. Meehan argued the evils of smoking per se, but he also viewed the debate as a forum for exposing the political influence of large tobacco companies. This is not unlike advocates of the 1993 Clinton health care plan who blamed years of inaction on the successful insurance lobbies. In a typical complaint, Meehan argued that "Congress comes up against the special interest money barrier every time we try to take on the tobacco industry as well. Public decisions and public policies are often abstract, but this one could not be clearer." A concern for public health, Meehan suggests, would have called for a strong rejection of tobacco long ago had tobacco donations (to Republicans in particular) not quieted these efforts. Getting such "walking money" out of the system would apparently open the gates for principled arguments about tobacco regulation to enter.

> Last year, Common Cause released a report that illustrated the enormous amount of money the tobacco industry pours into political campaigns to stop antitobacco legislation from passing. According to the report, tobacco giants like Philip Morris, R.J. Reynolds, U.S. Tobacco and the Tobacco Institute have donated millions of dollars to Members of Congress over the past 10 years. Without question, this report documents the way money in the form of campaign contributions influence[s] decisions that are made in Washington. (June 18, 1996, H6480)

Aside from Meehan's attempt to introduce a corruption angle into the debate, the advocates of instituting stricter tobacco control essentially found themselves with a single rhetorical strategy that focused on public health. Some emphasized children's health in particular. while many others warned of the risks of cigarettes—particularly nicotine as an addictive drug—for the entire population. Those who chose to speak on the issue often used personal experiences to motivate their arguments. Opponents of tobacco control used personal experiences as well, though they tended to justify the protection of small tobacco farms or constitutional liberties rather than the lives of those affected by tobacco smoke.

Rhetorical strategies reveal that members of Congress apparently allow their own values, interests, and histories to shape their stances toward tobacco legislation. The personalization of and simplification of issues was detected in the interviews described in chapter 2. Even on tobacco policy, those who spoke on the floor brought different reasonings with them to support their positions. Except in the strongest of partisan legislatures, we would not expect any less diversity of rhetoric. But their reasoning was striking in two respects.

First, in contrast to the complex language of the legislation itself, floor arguments were quite simple. Members tend not to present their colleagues and other interested observers of floor debate with many facts, summaries of technical reports, and hard data. Perhaps they do so a bit more frequently in committee, but even there the records of the members and those testifying do not suggest a great deal of detail. Instead, the arguments are more often about a fundamental idea or principle. Members boil down or otherwise frame the issue for greater portability. Many of the speeches were almost folksy in nature, suggesting that the divisions in Congress had less to do with the facts than their interpretation. Some of this is for show, to please constituents, lobbying groups, or other interested parties, thus justifying a simplifying of what could be a technical debate. But it also reflects the way that members of Congress actually speak to one another, and how they personally come to a position on an issue.

Second, these rather straightforward arguments were often built on a personal foundation and tended to be quite vivid. We might not necessarily expect members to make abstract appeals to partisanship or even ideology, since those are neither personally credible nor especially convincing. We would, however, expect appeals to policy principles, precedent, a view of the common good, or improving national welfare, yet even this does not happen much. Instead, one member tells us that his experience on a small, hillside tobacco farm convinces him that tobacco regulation is a bad idea. Another's father passed away because of a tobacco-induced battle with cancer. Several describe how they, their spouses, or other family members smoke or once smoked. Nearly every speech uses the pronoun "I." It is hard to know for certain whether these personal experiences are genuine motivation or simply rationalization. Either way, they suggest that members are apt to link policy choices with their own knowledge, values, and interests.

This combination of simplicity and personality counters the portrait painted by academics. Several decades ago junior members were constrained by roles, folkways, apprenticeship, and hierarchy such that their individuality was secondary to prescribed ways of acting. More recently it appears that interest group demands, partisanship, constituent pressure, or some more ethereal set of preferences drives activity, to the exclusion of other factors.[10] There is little place in either rubric for the legislator as person to emerge. Floor rhetoric suggests how this view might limit our understanding of legislators' motivations. Appreciating legislators as individuals is crucial to understanding their actions. The remainder of this chapter systematizes this appreciation with quantitative analyses of positions and participation on tobacco legislation in the House.

Where Members Stand and Why

A central assertion in this book is that appreciating *why* a member is located where he is (and with what *consequences)* is as important as knowing *where* he stands in the first place. The quantitative analysis starts with the last of these questions: positioning by legislators. After understanding why members take the positions they do on tobacco legislation, we can determine how those positions influence their level of participation in the legislative process.

I begin with multivariate models to explain roll call voting on tobacco bills. Two dependent variables of rather different scope are employed, both from the 104th Congress. One is an individual roll call vote, which has the benefit of being concrete and substantively meaningful, but the liability of being so policy-specific that idiosyncratic factors may play a disproportionate role in the outcome. The other measure is a general index of positioning on tobacco bills that, while lacking in substantive meaning, is perhaps more reliable because it combines an array of votes into a summary scale.

The specific vote is the House roll call on an amendment to H.R. 3603, an appropriations bill for the Department of Agriculture, the Food and Drug Administration (FDA), and other agencies with jurisdiction over tobacco regulation. The measure was House Amendment 1153, sponsored by antitobacco crusader Richard Durbin (D-IL). Its aim was to eliminate funding for agricultural extension programs related to tobacco farming, and to decimate tobacco crop insurance subsidies, a total cut of $25 million. This might not be much money in a $2 trillion budget, but it vitally important to some constituencies and symbolically important to many more. Most of the floor speeches excerpted above were centered around

[10] See Sinclair (1989) on changes in the Senate.

this controversial proposal. In a roll call on June 12, 1996, the Durbin amendment failed narrowly, 210–212.[11] We thus might expect such a vote to meet Krehbiel's (1999) standard: with a margin of just two votes, legislators' actions were indeed "outcome consequential."

More general positions on tobacco legislation are summarized by the SmokeFree Action ratings introduced above. As a scale of many items, it naturally represents a wider range of provisions relating to tobacco than does the narrower Durbin vote, allowing for finer gradations of positions among members. The two measures, different as they are, are used as dependent variables in identical regression models explaining positioning on tobacco policy. To isolate general positioning from the Durbin amendment, I exclude the Durbin vote from the SmokeFree Action score for each member. The score is simply recalculated for each member after removing the vote.

As these are the first of many such models presented in the book, I offer a fair amount of detail about the selection of explanatory variables. These variables represent three types of influences. First, there are district characteristics representing the interests of constituents and other players in the district (Krehbiel 1993a). Constituent interests will usually be taken as voters' ideological preferences, a close cousin of the partisan voting tendencies in a district. But a legislator might be particularly responsive to other actors such as prominent industries, religious organizations, local culture, occupational groupings, and the like. These groups tend to have sharper interests and are more attentive to the legislative process. To the degree that these variables have explanatory power, we shall conclude that members' operative positions have been induced by district interests of one kind or another.

In the case of tobacco policy I use three district factors. Voter Ideology is the general left-right orientation of voters as a measured by the share of the two-party presidential vote won by Bill Clinton in the 1996 election. Such a measure is a suitable proxy for something akin to the median voter in the district (Ansolabehere, Snyder, and Stewart 2001a; Burden 2004b; LeoGrande and Jeydel 1997). It is especially meaningful here given the clear antitobacco position taken by the Clinton administration. Two dummy variables indicate districts with a historical connection to tobacco. Regardless of one's moral or partisan feelings about smoking, tobacco issues might be viewed as an employment or cultural matter in parts of the country, say North Carolina or Virginia, where many families depend on jobs related to the growing, harvesting, and processing of the crop. South marks the 11 states that were part of the Confederacy and

[11] The vote did not fall strongly along party lines. The relationship between party affiliation and how a member voted is only marginally significant ($\chi^2 = 3.59, p = .06$).

known for being part of the "King Cotton" tradition. Because of its more traditional culture and uniquely conservative heritage, the South might produce legislators who are more protobacco (Erikson, Wright, and McIver 1993). Tobacco Industry Present indicates reliance on tobacco industry jobs. To be scored a 1, a tobacco company must employ at least 500 people in the district.[12] To the degree that tobacco is perceived as a jobs issue, the presence of the industry in a district should make the member more likely to oppose new tobacco regulations. While not a perfect measure, it is at least comparable across districts, since their populations are nearly equal. We should expect these variables to be meaningful predictors of positions if legislators are acting as instructed delegates. Via lobbying, each of these external factors could induce a legislator to take particular positions on tobacco legislation.

The second set of variables characterizes the legislator himself. This group includes two standard demographic variables, Black and Female, to allow for the possibility that African-Americans and women are disproportionately in favor of tobacco regulation. Such an orientation is suggested by the vast literatures on these two groups within Congress reviewed in chapter 2. Yet I expect these important demographic categories not to matter much in the tobacco context, particularly once other factors are controlled. Third, knowing whether or not a member herself smokes (Uses Tobacco), might help explain her tobacco positions (de Guia et al. 2003). While such a relationship could stem from pure self-interest, it is perhaps more likely to reflect experiences, values, and personal information that shape legislators' outlooks on tobacco policy. Fourth, Mormon legislators are identified with a dummy variable. Representatives who belong to the Latter Day Saints' church are likely to have internalized the church's prohibition on tobacco use and might be more likely to mobilize for further tobacco control.

Finally, I use the representative's Public Ideology as measured by the first dimension NOMINATE score. We would expect higher, more conservative values on the dimension to be associated with protobacco positions. While the most convenient and widely recognized measures of legislators' ideological positions are drawn from roll call votes, their use is tautologous. Jackson and Kingdon (1992) have shown that "explaining votes with votes" in this way jeopardizes inferences by overestimating the influence of ideology on the dependent variable, though other researchers are less concerned (Snyder 1992; Wright 1998). Although several ideol-

[12] These data come from *Congressional Districts in the 1990s* and include Brown & Williamson, Culbro, Liggett Group, Lorillard, Philip Morris, and RJR Nabisco. It is interesting to note that legislators from tobacco states like North Carolina tend to underestimate the number of deaths attributable to tobacco while legislators from non-tobacco states like Vermont tend to overestimate it (Goldstein et al. 1997).

ogy measures not based on roll calls exist for senators (Burden, Caldeira, and Groseclose 2000), they are more difficult to find for members of the House. Despite the problems of doing so, I include NOMINATE scores for members as rough indictors of their ideologies. Leaving out ideology would result in severe specification bias because of the omission of a theoretically important influence on legislative activity and thus might overestimate the influence of personal factors. Including a roll call–based ideology measure has the drawback of potentially overestimating the influence of left-right preferences. I prefer to err in this direction because it stacks the deck against finding other personal effects, rather than making them more likely due to omission biases. Regardless of the problems associated with each approach, the substantive results change surprisingly little when NOMINATE scores are added to or dropped from the models.

The third set of factors is institutional. These items capture the locations of the member in the chamber and the legislative process. First, to the degree that members self-select to committees based on their preferences, I include a dummy variable for members of the Health Subcommittee (of the Committee on Energy and Commerce), which has primary jurisdiction over tobacco policy in the House. We might expect those members to have strongly held opinions about tobacco policy. If "high demand" districts tend to send members to Health more often, as distributive models would suggest, then one might expect a negative coefficient on this variable, as districts with protobacco interests would monopolize seats on the panel. But it is easy to imagine that self-selection might instead lead to a bipolar distribution on the subcommittee of strong advocates and opponents of tobacco regulation (Maltzman 1999). The level of expertise in tobacco and public health matters that members of the subcommittee gain might push in one direction or the other as well. Second, I include a Freshman dummy variable. It identifies those members who have not had to deal with tobacco policy in the legislative process yet (Asher and Weisberg 1978; Kingdon 1989).

It is worth noting that the models do not include party affiliation. Adding a party dummy does not change the results much, but there are good reasons for excluding it, not the least of which is the nearly perfect correlation with NOMINATE (r = .91).[13] I expect that some of the relationships explored below will be conditional on party. Specifically, the underlying models will be different for Democrats and Republicans, so that variables important for one group might not be for the other. To keep the models relatively consistent, I omit partisanship from them all.

[13] Somewhat surprisingly, no variables in either model go from being significant to insignificant and vice versa when a party dummy is included.

Table 3.2 presents the results of the multivariate regression analyses. Positions on the Durbin amendment and SmokeFree Action scores are modeled as a function of the three kinds of variables. The left column uses logit analysis to explain voting on the amendment, while the right column uses two-limit tobit to explain members' SmokeFree Action scores since

TABLE 3.2
Tobacco Bill Roll Call Votes

	H.Amdt. 1153 Vote	*SmokeFree Action Score*
Tobacco Industry Present	−2.20*	−34.25**
	(1.22)	(10.95)
Voter Ideology	1.83	−26.50
	(1.72)	(21.50)
South	−1.11**	−19.88**
	(.25)	(3.35)
Black	−.99*	.71
	(.56)	(7.15)
Female	.71*	5.76
	(.37)	(4.61)
Uses Tobacco	−.30	−16.85**
	(.49)	(6.74)
Mormon	−.87	13.81
	(.84)	(8.74)
Public Ideology	−.60*	−57.85**
	(.30)	(4.03)
Health Subcommittee	.33	−1.50
	(.49)	(6.35)
Freshman	.17	2.13
	(.28)	(3.80)
Constant	−.43	66.82**
	(.78)	(9.81)
σ		27.65**
		(1.26)
Log Likelihood	−253.10	−1470.50
Number of Cases	410	427

Note: Cell entries in left column are logit coefficients with standard errors in parentheses. Cell entries in right column are tobit coefficients with standard errors in parentheses. SmokeFree Action score excludes the Durbin amendment vote.
$^{*}p < .05$, $^{**}p < .01$, one-tailed test.

the measure is bounded at 0 and 100 (Tobin 1958). In both models higher values indicate positions that are more procontrol (i.e., antitobacco).

The results indicate that several factors shape reactive positioning on tobacco policy. First, ideological predispositions appear to play a large role in determining how a legislator votes on tobacco measures. Proxies for personal preferences such as ideology and region have clear effects as conservatives and southerners have significantly lower SmokeFree Action scores. Second, there is discernable district influence on representatives' tobacco records, but it comes in the form of economics rather than ideology. There is no evidence that voters' ideological leanings affect how their representatives vote. In contrast, legislators representing districts where tobacco companies are major employers are much less likely to support antitobacco legislation. This may be a proxy for the opinions of protobacco subconstituencies or indicate the influence of tobacco business interests in the district. Generally speaking, the results produce a rather conventional political science portrait of the determinants of roll call votes. The only clear anomaly is that district ideology has no effect once other variables have been controlled.

The finding that a legislator's ideology is powerful is not especially surprising, although we cannot be sure whether the effect is due to principled philosophical choices or just a desire for consistency over time. This is, after all, a measure based on roll call votes just like the dependent variable. With this variable included, it now seems that differences between smokers and nonsmokers shown earlier in figure 3.3 are only partly the product of ideology and the economic interests of the district. When the SmokeFree Action score is included in the analysis, personal tobacco use is a significant predictor of a member's roll call votes on tobacco control, although the vote on the Durbin amendment seems not to depend on tobacco use, all in all a modest effect. What happens when the analysis shifts from reactive roll call votes to proactive speeches and sponsorships is an open question.

Moving Rather than Standing

Were roll call voting all that one cared about, the analysis would end here. However, the theory offered in chapter 2 expects that members' motivations will be quite different when they are participating proactively than when reactively. Perhaps contrary to what democratic theorists might desire, legislators' personal interests become more important for those who believe their interests are threatened. District interests tied to the policy will also encourage proactive participation. These members tend to mobilize to defend the status quo.

Reactive policy measures are easy to find. Hundreds of roll call votes come down the pike each year. What is peculiar about roll calls is that they are determined by a small number of party and committee leaders, and the votes themselves are utterly egalitarian. Regardless of the intensity of their preferences or interest in the issue, every member gets an equal say in whether the measure is approved or not. In most cases members have no choice but to take a side, even if they would prefer not to do so.

Proactive participation is another matter. As Hall (1996) has demonstrated so well, participation is costly and selective. Members must choose just a few battles, and each policy front sees only a limited number of representatives active. Hall shows that members tend to pick policy areas in which they have some investment (such as specialized knowledge from committee work) or a personal interest. I add the expectation that such factors (and others that I add) are also correlated with the *side* of the debate on which a member finds himself. It is not just that members become proactive on an issue, but their tendency to do so is a product of whether they are for or against a change to the status quo. Precisely how this correlation between activity level and position manifests itself is examined below.

I measure a member's proactivity on a policy in two ways: cosponsorship and floor speeches. Bill sponsorship is a fairly important activity as legislative matters go: it puts a member on record and attracts attention to a bill (Koger 2003; Schiller 1995). Each bill has a primary sponsor and an unlimited number of cosponsors. Members are frequently asked by colleagues to sponsor bills, usually in the form of impersonal "Dear Colleague" letters. Interest groups and party leaders will also urge members to cosponsor (or not to cosponsor) particular bills. There is also a great deal of variation in the tendency to cosponsor. Speeches are a different breed of proactive behavior. They are less frequent—the highest number by any one member being just six in the 104th Congress—and are less immediate than sponsoring a bill. As more symbolic behavior aimed at constituents, floor speeches are not expected to follow the same defensive patterns as cosponsorships, which should be more closely connected to those defending the status quo.

My approach differs from the general participation scales created by Hall (1996) and Wawro (2001a). I analyze speeches and sponsorships separately and distinguish activities that are *for* a proposal from those that are *against* it.[14] I begin with cosponsorship of tobacco-related legislation in the 104th Congress. Here the dependent variable is the number of bills either pro- or anti-tobacco that a member cosponsored. I am not concerned with activity per se but the "mobilization of bias" that it reflects. The explanatory variables remain the same as in the roll call analy-

[14] In addition, Wawro includes only primary sponsors while I focus on all cosponsors.

sis above, but this is not because I expect the same relationships to hold. Indeed, the point is to show how district interests and legislator's characteristics take on differing levels of importance in determining proactive as distinguished from reactive participation. Only one variable—Total Cosponsorships—is added to the regression to control for a member's baseline propensity to be involved with many kinds legislation.

The count models in table 3.3 show that proactive and reactive policy actions, while sharing some baseline factors, are also driven by rather different sets of forces. Those acting in favor of tobacco regulation are doing so for different reasons than those acting in opposition. Of greatest interest are the effects of having a tobacco company in the district or personally using tobacco. As might be expected, members from tobacco districts tend not to advocate for tobacco regulation, and they actively sponsor bills to avoid further regulation. But members who use tobacco are disproportionately likely to cosponsor antiregulation bills. Likewise, being Mormon has a bigger depressing effect on protobacco sponsorship than it enhances antitobacco sponsorship. Religion showed no effects on roll call voting, but Mormonism turns up as an important explanatory variable once the analysis focuses on proactive rather than reactive behavior. Contrary to most of the literature, constituent ideology continues to have no effect on legislative action on tobacco.

What appeared to be a null effect of membership on the relevant committee in the roll call analysis above has asymmetric effects when it comes to proactive legislating. Members of the Health Subcommittee are no more likely than nonmembers to cosponsor new regulations but are significantly less likely to sign onto bills opposing tobacco regulation. While the vote analysis did not show the committee to be unrepresentative of the chamber's interests, this study of proactive behavior finds significant and asymmetric influence consistent with "high demand" members. At this point we cannot determine whether this bias is due to self-selection or the additional information one learns by virtue of serving on a committee.

For both theoretical and methodological reasons, the results in table 3.3 do not include party affiliation. Not only is the collinearity with public ideology too great for the model to sustain, but I suspect that partisanship has more subtle and systemic effects than a dummy variable can reveal. My argument suggests that the effects of the other variables may be conditional on party.[15] Table 3.4 thus repeats the analysis separately for Democrats and Republicans.[16]

[15] See also Heckman and Snyder's (1997) argument that the first dimension NOMINATE score is merely a "stand in" for party.

[16] The effects of race on Republican behavior are really those of Representative J. C. Watts (R-OK) who was the only black Republican in the House at the time.

TABLE 3.3
Tobacco Bill Cosponsorship, by Position

	Against Tobacco Regulation	*For Tobacco Regulation*
Tobacco Industry Present	1.66**	−13.27*
	(.41)	(.62)
Voter Ideology	1.72	−.46
	(1.94)	(1.64)
South	1.27**	−.53
	(.31)	(.45)
Black	.34	−1.08*
	(.71)	(.51)
Female	−.68	.05
	(.70)	(.31)
Uses Tobacco	.88**	−.41
	(.32)	(.68)
Mormon	−13.20**	2.80**
	(.44)	(.79)
Public Ideology	1.10*	−2.21**
	(.50)	(.39)
Health Subcommittee	−1.45*	−.60
	(.65)	(.85)
Freshman	.31	−.75
	(.29)	(.48)
Total Cosponsorships	−.0002	.01**
	(.002)	(.001)
Constant	−3.54**	−3.18**
	(.98)	(.95)
Log Likelihood	−175.75	−175.04
Number of Cases	425	

Note: Cell entries are Poisson regression coefficients with robust standard errors in parentheses.

* $p < .05$, ** $p < .01$, one-tailed test.

TABLE 3.4
Tobacco Bill Cosponsorship, by Position and Party

	Against Tobacco Regulation		*For Tobacco Regulation*	
	Democrat	*Republican*	*Democrat*	*Republican*
Tobacco Industry Present	1.70** (.55)	1.15* (.51)	−14.68** (.60)	4.48* (2.57)
Voter Ideology	−1.72 (3.01)	7.81** (2.79)	.15 (1.41)	−16.39 (11.58)
South	2.08** (.88)	.77** (.33)	−.41 (.49)	−22.00** (.81)
Black	.42 (1.03)	2.31** (.35)	−1.10* (.48)	−22.28** (2.71)
Female	−1.03 (1.03)	.04 (.81)	−.12 (.30)	.26 (1.22)
Uses Tobacco	.75* (.37)	1.55** (.44)	−.38 (.69)	−21.01** (1.07)
Mormon	−14.24** (1.32)	−14.81** (.51)	1.56 (1.04)	4.26* (1.86)
Public Ideology	.73 (.64)	6.31** (1.16)	−2.32** (.81)	−11.17** (3.91)
Health Subcommittee	−14.26** (.63)	−1.51* (.76)	−.53 (.82)	−21.38** (.93)
Cosponsorships	−.003 (.003)	.003 (.003)	.008** (.001)	.004 (.006)
Freshman	.94 (.61)	.22 (.31)	−.53 (.49)	−.76 (1.58)
Constant	−2.00 (1.97)	−10.15** (1.74)	−3.56** (.93)	8.07* (4.75)
Log Likelihood	−59.65	−98.28	−134.89	−27.76
Number of Cases	196	228	196	228

Note: Cell entries are Poisson regression coefficients with robust standard errors in parentheses.

* $p < .05$, ** $p < .01$, one-tailed test.

The results tell a complicated story. For some variables, the important distinction is whether one is for or against tobacco control. For example, regardless of party, Mormon representatives are much less likely than their colleagues to sponsor a bill that protects tobacco. For several other variables the effects depend on an interaction between party and position. Consider the effects of having a substantial tobacco company located in one's district. Members from tobacco districts are more likely to be a cosponsor, both for and against tobacco control, except for Democrats, who are significantly less likely to advocate tobacco regulations. Legislators who smoke are more likely to sponsor bills opposed to tobacco regulation, regardless of their party affiliation. Among those supporting regulation, tobacco use is significant only for Republicans, who are less likely to sponsor.

The other proactive measure I consider is the floor speech. While much of the floor debate consists of symbolic actions rather than genuine attempts to change colleagues' opinions, speeches differ from cosponsorships in an important way. Many members sign on to a bill as a cosponsor because they are asked by a colleague. Although each member is autonomous and might seek out a bill to add his support, an invitation from someone else often makes it happen. Speeches, on the other hand, are typically made (or not made) because the member chooses. And while a party might provide talking points or encourage its members to participate on the floor, there is more evidence of individual intent in decisions about giving speeches than in cosponsoring, if only because speeches require more effort. Although they are more selective activities, speeches are not necessarily more consequential.

I repeat the analysis of cosponsorships, now substituting the number of protobacco or antitobacco floor speeches made by a member during the 104th Congress. Despite the theoretical differences between sponsorship and speechmaking, the results from the two regressions mirror one another quite closely. Table 3.5 shows that members' tobacco use only affects antitobacco speechmaking, with smokers being much less likely than nonsmokers to give speeches in favor of tobacco regulation. Similarly, having a tobacco company in one's district is a much more powerful predictor of antitobacco speeches (where again members from tobacco country are unlikely to give a speech). A representative's public ideology, as indicated by the NOMINATE score, also appears to have more affect on proregulation speeches than antiregulation speeches. One variable that works in the other direction is constituent ideology, which is only a robust influence on antiregulation speeches. The more important result for our purposes is the double-barreled finding that personal interests are more likely to animate proactive than reactive behavior and that the proactive motivations are not equal and opposite in effect for the pro and anti forces.

TABLE 3.5
Tobacco Floor Speeches

	Against Tobacco Regulation	*For Tobacco Regulation*
Tobacco Industry Present	1.50**	−14.41**
	(.47)	(.61)
Voter Ideology	7.06**	−1.07
	(2.00)	(2.94)
South	1.93**	−1.33*
	(.48)	(.73)
Black	−1.09	−2.15
	(.76)	(1.31)
Female	−.69	.62
	(.72)	(.51)
Uses Tobacco	.69	−13.72**
	(.64)	(.47)
Mormon	−13.71**	2.21**
	(.54)	(.87)
Public Ideology	.90*	−2.17**
	(.51)	(.63)
Health Subcommittee	−1.22	1.16
	(.95)	(.78)
Freshman	.82*	.84*
	(.49)	(.49)
Constant	−6.40**	−2.17
	(1.01)	(1.49)
Log Likelihood	−173.85	−119.98
Number of Cases	427	

Note: Cell entries are Poisson regression coefficients with robust standard errors in parentheses.
*$p < .05$, ** $p < .01$, one-tailed test.

As was done for cosponsorships, the speech results are broken down by party in table 3.6. Once again personal factors and asymmetries emerge. In deciding whether or not to give a speech, having a tobacco company in the district makes members of both parties more likely to say something on the floor in opposition to regulation. But a company presence makes only Democrats less likely to give a floor speech favoring regulation. This is an another interactive effect of party and position. In contrast, personal tobacco use has nothing to do with party and everything to do with one's position. Smokers are far less likely than nonsmokers to give speeches advocating tobacco regulation, but they are no more likely to give antiregulation addresses. Partisanship appears to play no direct role, as tobacco use itself is suppressing speechmaking in favor of regulation.

Among other finds, district ideology plays a surprisingly limited role in speechmaking. Only Republicans defending tobacco appear responsive to voters' ideological views. A final result of interest has to do with committee membership. Members of the Health Subcommittee are no more likely than other members to give speeches opposing further regulation of tobacco. But committee membership is a predictor of speeches given in favor of regulation, with Democrats giving significantly more speeches and Republicans giving far fewer. This is rough evidence for bipolar committee preferences that translate quite readily into proactive behavior.

Consequences

To this point interest groups have been omitted from the analyses. Although their influence was permitted through a dummy variable marking districts that contain sizable tobacco firms, direct lobbying by tobacco companies has been assumed to be ineffective. This omission might be consequential since lobbying by tobacco companies is a potential form of persuasion. In addition to the factors already accounted for in the regression models, it is possible that the tobacco lobby could induce members to act on their behalf. Yet I did not include protobacco PAC donations in the above models because campaign contributions are not exogenous "causes" of legislative behavior. Just as interest groups lobby members who already agree with them (Hall and Deardorff 2006), PACs tend to donate to allies to mobilize and maintain access to them rather than "buy" votes (Hall 1996; Wright 1996), even in the tobacco arena (Sharfstein 1998; Wilkerson and Carrell 1999; Wright 1998). Empirically, there is a positive relationship between legislative voting in the direction a PAC prefers and contributions from the PAC, but this is far from demonstrating that interest groups can purchase roll call votes, since the relationship often vanishes under proper specification (Chappell 1982; Wawro 2001b). Although other forms of lobbying could influence legislators simply by providing them with information (Hall and Deardorff 2006), modest campaign donations should not be particularly effective.

Even if one believes that roll call votes, bill cosponsorship, and floor speeches have little impact on public opinion or public policy, it is quite possible that interest groups respond to such actions. This would be consequential since the PAC arms of interest groups can make campaign con-

TABLE 3.6
Tobacco Floor Speeches, by Party

	Against Tobacco Regulation		*For Tobacco Regulation*	
	Democrat	*Republican*	*Democrat*	*Republican*
Tobacco Industry Present	1.43**	1.92*	−15.79**	−1.12
	(.56)	(.97)	(.66)	(1.09)
Voter Ideology	3.01	13.11**	−3.40	11.06
	(3.70)	(3.69)	(2.94)	(16.12)
South	1.92**	.80	−.67	−15.72**
	(.76)	(.62)	(.88)	(.57)
Black	−.06	−24.50**	−1.95	−18.68**
	(1.17)	(1.15)	(1.30)	(1.63)
Female	−.25	−16.07**	.31	1.51
	(.78)	(.51)	(.64)	(1.08)
Uses Tobacco	.16	1.26	−16.07**	−16.80**
	(.97)	(.96)	(.64)	(.76)
Mormon	−13.98**	−17.98**	−15.06**	2.93**
	(1.14)	(.68)	(1.49)	(.67)
Public Ideology	1.98**	4.08*	−4.78**	−1.66
	(.57)	(1.99)	(1.94)	(2.57)
Health Subcommittee	−14.01**	−1.25	1.60*	−18.15**
	(.60)	(1.67)	(.93)	(.91)
Cosponsorships	.001	−.007	.001	−.01
	(.003)	(.005)	(.003)	(.01)
Freshman	1.51**	.44	.60	.85
	(.46)	(.54)	(1.03)	(.76)
Constant	−4.26*	−9.55**	−2.76	−5.90
	(2.18)	(2.47)	(2.01)	(7.93)
Log Likelihood	−76.30	−69.76	−77.07	−29.95
Number of Cases	196	228	196	228

Note: Cell entries are Poisson regression coefficients with robust standard errors in parentheses.

*$p < .05$, ** $p < .01$, one-tailed test.

tributions to reward members who act in their interests. I open up the possibility that PACs and other donors and activists carefully monitor behavior in their policy domain and then spend resources to favor members who act on the "right" side of the issue. This could be done to maintain access or even to buy votes, but the literature suggests that most money is given to keep incumbents in office by deterring or defeating strong challengers (Box-Steffensmeier 1996). A strong war chest allows an incumbent to ward off challengers, which, I noted in chapter 2, limits the ability of voters to use elections as instruments of policy control.

From my point of view, it is more theoretically justifiable to explain PAC donations in terms of legislative behavior than the other way around. I estimate a simple model of PAC contributions, using many of the same explanatory variables used above. The dependent variable indicates the amount of money contributed to the legislator by several protobacco PACs.[17] As independent variables I carry over the same factors used in the models above, adding both reactive and proactive measures of participation on tobacco legislation.

In addition to the variables that have been used in the models thus far, I also include the dependent variables from those models as independent variables here. Tobacco PAC donations could respond to the same forces that members' own actions depend on, but PACs might also pay special attention to votes, cosponsorships, and speeches.

Table 3.7 presents the OLS regression results.[18] The first column presents general results for all members; the next two columns separate the results by party. Again, some factors matter regardless of partisanship. Members who give speeches opposed to further tobacco control receive about $2,000 more on average from tobacco PACs. Likewise, those with voting records opposed to tobacco company interests get less in the way of contributions, although the relationship is stronger for Republicans than Democrats. A decrease in 10 points on the SmokeFree Action scale would net Democrats $550 more from tobacco PACS but would earn Republicans $905 more.

In addition to this modest result, many more variables depend on party. Most interesting for our purposes are the effects of legislators' tobacco use. Republicans who smoke receive almost $4,000 more in PAC donations, while Democrats who smoke actually get almost $1,500 less. Tobacco PACs apparently consider district ideology more when giving (or not giving) to Democrats, but for Republicans are more sensitive to whether tobacco companies are located in their districts. Surprisingly, Republicans who represent tobacco districts get less, not more, in tobacco PAC donations. This might represent an attempt by tobacco interests to buy the vote of unsympathetic Republicans. Finally, Republicans but not Democrats on the Health Subcommittee get nearly $3,000 more in contributions. Had this analysis followed convention by merely inserting a

[17] These data were compiled and published by SmokeFree Action.

[18] While one might be inclined to use a tobit or selection model due to the large number of zeros (Sigelman and Zeng 2000), there are also negative values in the data where checks were returned to PACs, among other reasons, so I stick with linear regression. The substantive results are robust to the model chosen.

TABLE 3.7
Explaining Tobacco PAC Contributions to House Incumbents

	All Members	*Democrats*	*Republicans*
South	−777.27 (538.02)	−1659.98* (670.35)	−165.72 (777.22)
Tobacco Industry Present	−329.72 (1778.32)	258.48 (1962.41)	−6077.06* (3260.25)
Voter Ideology	−4844.46* (2695.51)	−5870.59* (3042.16)	−1582.29 (5302.18)
Black	6.12 (629.80)	603.13 (608.35)	−104.39 (1066.91)
Female	−724.53* (403.58)	−1041.84* (481.03)	266.04 (628.56)
Uses Tobacco	1896.58 (1540.45)	−1446.05* (685.66)	3936.97* (2242.44)
Mormon	−131.09 (970.17)	−2851.38** (701.66)	718.06 (1197.15)
Public Ideology	−2603.65* (1489.15)	−1985.67 (1899.22)	−987.75 (2614.20)
Party	529.32 (1254.54)		
Health Subcommittee	1739.52* (946.33)	231.96 (783.51)	2917.59* (1434.02)
Freshman	538.33 (522.52)	218.05 (1023.06)	496.25 (588.89)
For Regulation Cosponsorships	−314.50* (166.89)	−358.91* (175.37)	−406.63 (374.02)
Against Regulation Cosponsorships	1748.35** (689.06)	2613.01* (1166.95)	545.83 (986.61)
For Regulation Speeches	150.14 (172.88)	92.91 (111.98)	432.46 (1024.12)
Against Regulation Speeches	2144.07** (288.09)	2066.70** (294.16)	2617.68** (1024.12)
Smokefree Action score	−67.02** (9.50)	−54.72** (11.95)	−90.50** (14.61)
Constant	7436.00** (1824.02)	8343.49** (1758.33)	6541.32* (3160.71)
R^2	.38	.50	.31
Number of Cases	422	197	225

Note: Cell entries are OLS regression coefficients with robust standard errors in parentheses.

$^*p < .10$, $^{**}p < .05$, one-tailed test.

party dummy variable into the model, one would have concluded that PAC contributions are unresponsive to partisanship. Dividing members by party shows just how dependent on party PACs' behavior is.

This conditionality also relates to members' proactive legislative behaviors. For example, cosponsoring bills can bring in more or less tobacco money for Democrats, but not for Republicans. Among Democrats, every proregulation bill sponsored costs them less than $400, but every antiregulation cosponsorship earns them a whopping $2,600. Speeches, in contrast, earn legislators greater donations regardless of party. In short, not only do a wide variety of traits and interests affect legislators' proactive behavior, but they predict in part how interest groups decide to support or oppose particular members. Moreover, many of the same asymmetries that showed up in the analyses of representatives' actions are apparent in even this limited model of PAC motivations.

It is intriguing that tobacco PACs seem to reward more than punish, at least when it comes to proactive behavior. There is little evidence that the tobacco industry is any less likely to give to members who act against them (though one should beware of floor effects). There is consistent evidence that PACs shower money on those who work on their behalf in the House. Cosponsoring a protobacco industry bill or making a speech brings in about $2,000 each time it is done. This is a substantial effect since PAC contributions were limited to $5,000 per candidate per election at the time and most groups gave far less than the maximum. Likewise, voting is watched closely, albeit with much smaller ramifications. Even a dramatic shift of 20 points on the SmokeFree Action scale would raise or lower tobacco company donations by roughly $1,300. And this, unlike a speech or cosponsorship, is not an easily repeated activity and is not selective. The point is that financial backers also act asymmetrically and reward proactive behavior more than reactive behavior. The same activities on the other side of the issue seem to exact no penalties. And it appears all the more potent since antitobacco activities are consistently more likely to be motivated by the interests of members and their districts.

Conclusion

This chapter has presented the first and most extensive of three policy case studies. After providing evidence on the ways in which tobacco interests became politically relevant in the 1990s, I demonstrated how district and legislator interests affected behavior in the 104th House. These interests were more likely to affect proactive behaviors—speechmaking and cosponsoring—than reactive roll call votes. Moreover, the influence was generally asymmetric in that those aligned with tobacco were more likely to be motivated by personal interests than those pushing for change, particularly as the analysis shifted upstream from roll call votes to speeches and then to bill sponsorship. Finally, proactive behavior opposed to tobacco regulation was rewarded by protobacco donors, whereas antitobacco action was not punished, and PACs were more responsive to proactive than reactive behavior.

CHAPTER FOUR

Vouchers and School Choice

EDUCATION REFORM HAS BEEN HIGH on the public agenda in recent years, frequently becoming a source of debate on the presidential campaign trail and in the halls of Congress. Public education expenditures are a matter of serious partisan debate, but so too are the principles that undergird public schools. The traditional public school system has come under greater scrutiny, and the 1990s saw a rising challenge to the educational status quo. The principles of choice and accountability were given new emphasis. Among other proposals, charter schools and private school vouchers were offered as options to students in underperforming schools.[1]

Confronting as it did existing educational policy frameworks, the school reform movement often divided the Left from the Right. Most liberals today believe that tuition vouchers are a bad idea because they undermine universal public education, an institution the Democrats have long supported. Some conservatives oppose vouchers because they represent further government interference in local education, although the vast majority of those on the right favor the idea of marketplace choice. Competition is thus valued by reformers who believe that choice is a fundamental right, but it is opposed by those believe that the withdrawal of voucher-supported students from public schools would weaken the system and harm students who remain. School choice proposals fascinate because they tap into more abstract notions about the role of government in providing public goods and specific views about private and public school performance.

In this chapter I show that members of Congress face these same dueling concerns when they take action on education policy, particularly on voucher programs. In addition to ideological and partisan considerations, legislators make educational choices for the country and their own children that reflect their values, interests, and expertise about school options. I show that these choices shape preferences and action on school choice

[1] School choice and vouchers are technically separate proposals, though they are often considered together. School choice simply permits students to attend (typically public) schools of their choice (within some geographic limits) and do not tend to be means-tested. Vouchers (or "tuitioning" programs) provide funds for students in public schools to put toward private school tuition and are likely to be means-tested. Gallup surveys from the early 2000s show a roughly equal number of respondents in favor of and opposed to voucher programs.

legislation. In this chapter I first document how changes in education policy have threatened defenders of the traditional public school system in recent years and then demonstrate how this challenge interacts with personal choices to produce legislative action.

Changes in Education Politics

Even after the creation of the Department of Education in 1979, education policy and funding remained largely a state and local matter. States maintained their own public universities and through local officials managed vast arrays of elementary, secondary, and vocational schools. Policies concerning teacher credentials, student assessment, and funding were often decided locally by school boards. This is still an accurate description of the public school system in America today. Claims that American schools were lagging behind those of other nations, were too bureaucratic, were unaccountable, and at times were unsafe resonated with many policymakers and yet were difficult to broach at the national level because the existing public school system was accountable to parents and local administrators.

Changes in education policy have been afoot since at least the 1980s. But it was the 1990s that saw an explosion of experimentation with school choice and an enhanced federal role in education policy. Policymakers who endorsed some version of the existing public school system were put on the defensive. One indicator of the strength of the status quo is federal spending on education, which illustrates the threats afoot. As figure 4.1 shows, federal spending on education increased quite dramatically from the 1960s until the Reagan administration. This growth, which was paralleled as the state level, helped establish the public school system. Reagan's budget cuts upset the status quo by withdrawing federal support. Even by the end of the Clinton years federal spending had not returned to its pre-1980 levels.

From the civil rights era onward, Democrats pushed for greater federal support for public education; Republicans followed, albeit reluctantly and usually with an emphasis on local control. To alleviate stress on inner city schools and reduce class sizes, Bill Clinton's 1998 State of the Union address called for the hiring of 100,000 new teachers nationwide. After some initial resistance, Republicans capitulated, and the plan was signed into law in 1999 as part of the federal budget. Despite Clinton's victory, Republicans continued to advocate local administration and funding of schools.

As concerns grew about inner city schools in particular, dissatisfied policymakers looked for alternatives to the traditional public school. An

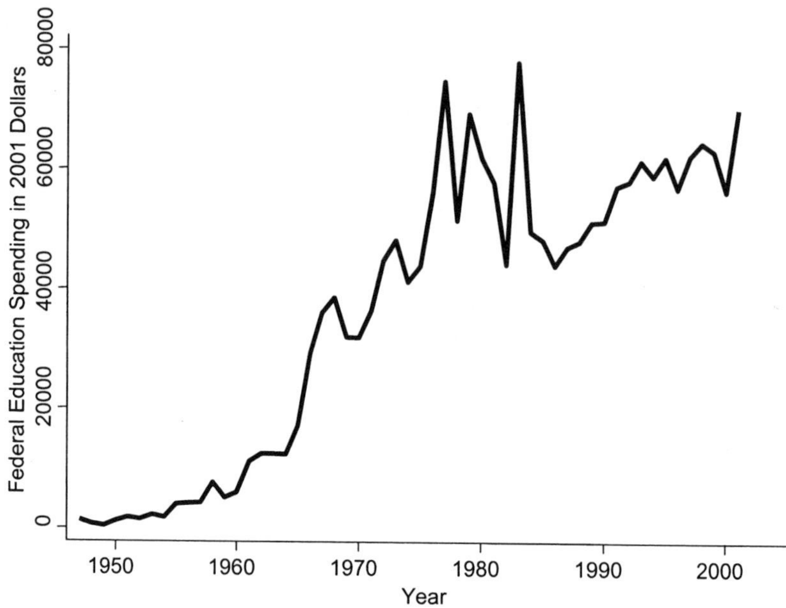

Figure 4.1. Federal spending on education (1947–2001). *Note:* Data are taken from the Policy Agendas Project. Spending is measured in constant FY2001 dollars.

early option appeared in the form of the charter school. Charter schools are publicly funded, but face fewer restrictions on curricula in exchange for sharper expectations about student performance. Initially the idea was thought to unite the Left and the Right by granting both more autonomy and more accountability. Some hoped that charter schools would encourage innovation in the classroom. Charter proponents emphasized choice and competition, believing that new schools' flexibility would improve the educational marketplace for all students. Minnesota passed a charter school law in 1991, and other states quickly created their own charter school legislation. The federal government began subsidizing these efforts in 1994, and President Clinton pushed for the creation of 3,000 charter schools in his 1997 State of the Union speech. Some 40 states now allow for charters in one way or another, and enrollment has grown rapidly. Although traditional public schools continue to dominate the educational market, charter schools are unique because they play by different rules and are the fasting-growing type of school. The rise of the charter school is seen by many as sign of the challenges that existing public schools face (Finn, Manno, and Vanourek 2001).

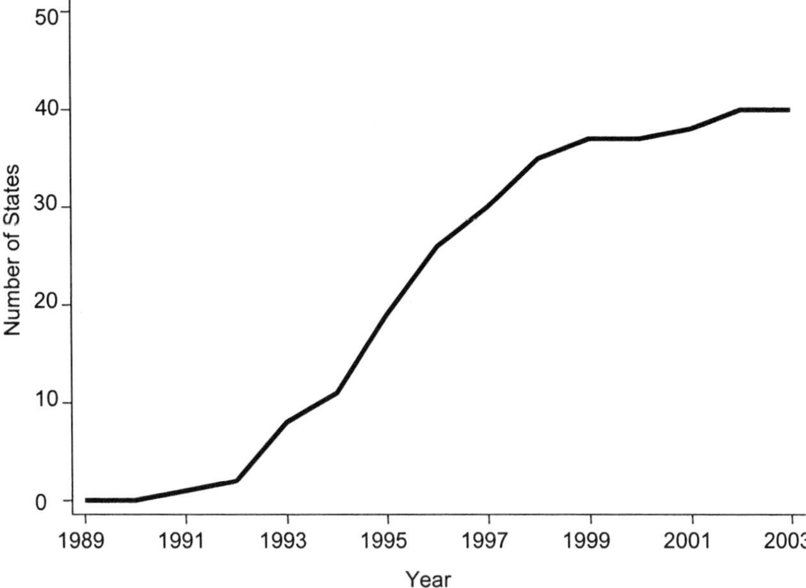

Figure 4.2. Number of states with charter school laws (1989–2003). Includes Washington, DC. *Source:* Center for Education Reform.

As figure 4.2 shows, the number of states allowing charter schools grew tremendously in the 1990s. In 1990 not a single state had passed a law recognizing charter schools; within a decade nearly 40 states had done so. In a short period of time charter schools were being created at a rapid pace. Figure 4.3 shows that only a couple hundred charters existed as late as the 1995–96 academic year. But several hundred new charter schools appeared every year, reaching a total of over 2,000 just 10 years after the first state legislated their creation.[2]

A more direct type of school choice has been urged in the form of private school vouchers. Vouchers allow students in unsafe or underperforming public schools to attend private schools of their choice. Vouchers can be delivered in the form of direct payments of a few thousand dollars or as a tax credit or deduction for parents who pay private school tuition. There have been proposals to implement a nationwide voucher system, but practically speaking vouchers have only gotten off the ground in an

[2] The National Center for Education Statistics estimates a smaller number of charter schools than does the Center for Education Reform, but the upward trends in both sets of estimates are identical.

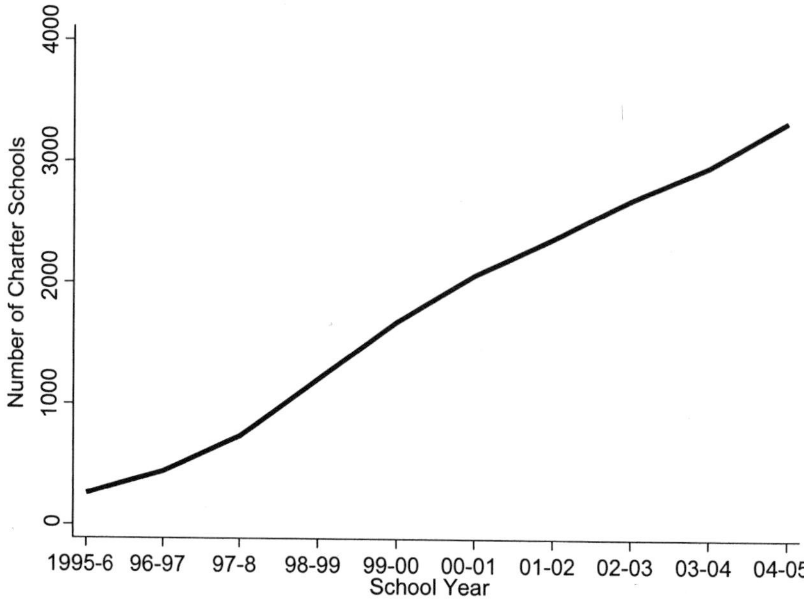

Figure 4.3. Number of charter schools (1995–2005). *Source:* Center for Education Reform.

experimental way in a few cities. Milwaukee became one of the first voucher communities in 1990, giving students below a defined income threshold as much as $5,882 to pay private school tuition. Cleveland adopted a less generous version of this plan in 1996, offering parents partial support in the form of $2,000 vouchers. A voucher experiment was implemented by a private organization in New York in 1997, offering vouchers of $1,400 for each of three years. By the late 1990s, Dayton, San Antonio, and Washington, DC, were also among the cities experimenting with private school vouchers.

Voucher plans raise a larger set of issues than do charter school proposals because they allow private schools to compete more directly with public schools. Charter schools also provide choice, competition, and innovation, but do so within the public realm. Vouchers introduce the private sector, which raises at least three other considerations. First, unlike public schools, private schools are rarely unionized. Teacher unions such as the National Education Association (NEA) are naturally concerned that private school teachers will earn less and have inadequate credentials. Second, because most private schools have religious affiliations, vouchers highlight the tension between church and state. Many people dislike the idea of spending public funds to subsidize religious enterprises even if the courts have shown a willingness to allow the practice. In contrast, parochial school parents already paying tuition bills might happily accept reimbursement for at least some of their expenses. Third, because private schools and public schools have traditionally served different socioeconomic and racial groups, vouchers are sometimes viewed as a mechanism for market-based racial integration. Surveys have shown that blacks, who are otherwise liberal and Democratic in orientation, tend to favor vouchers as least as much as their more conservative white counterparts. For some, vouchers are a way to improve the plight of urban minorities who suffer in unsafe or ill-equipped public school systems. Others believe that "creaming" (as it is called by school policymakers) will draw away better-off white students, leaving behind disadvantaged minority students with weaker performance.

The long-lived consensus supporting American public elementary and secondary education began to crack in the 1990s. Federal spending in the post-Reagan era never returned to earlier levels. Alternatives to the traditional system were seriously entertained and funded at the local level. When Republicans won control of Congress in 1994, these choice-oriented experiments received even more attention, as the very existence of the Department of Education was challenged. Moreover, resistance to public sector teachers' unions became stronger. Nonunionized alternatives such as charter schools tapped into public resources, as did many of the proposed voucher programs. Supporters of the status quo—mainly pro-public-sector Democrats—saw new threats to the existing system, while free-market conservatives viewed the new ideas as exciting opportunities to improve elementary and secondary school education.

Alert to changes on the horizon, members of Congress were required to take action on school policy in this new environment. Defenders of the public school system felt pressure to protect the existing structure; reformers faced the burden of demonstrating the promise of a privatized system, hence the push for experimental pilot programs. Partisanship naturally played a heavy role in these policy debates, but members of Congress also violated their parties' positions at times or voluntarily chose to become more involved with particular bills. These choices frequently stemmed from their own values, expertise, or self-interest, much of which drew upon personal contact with educational institutions. Unlike other issues, education touches everyone because many members of Congress have been teachers, most have children, and all were students at one time. I will show that legislators' decisions were determined nearly as much by their personal experiences with public and private schools as their ideological orientations and cues from constituents and other external forces. In particular, I demonstrate that even after controlling for other variables, representatives with children in private school were more likely to support school choice, while those with children in public school were more likely to support the status quo. Much of the floor rhetoric concerning school choice also reflected these personal choices. In addition, campaign contributions from teachers' unions showed sensitivity to members' backgrounds.

Data Sources

I begin with information about the choices that legislators made about schools for their children. In early 2000 the Heritage Foundation conducted a survey of members of Congress to determine whether or not legislators had school-age children and, if so, whether they sent them to public or private schools.[3] The House survey earned a high response rate (86%) because Heritage researchers asked staff in each office if the member had any children who were school-age and whether their children attended or had ever attended private schools. The survey revealed that the overwhelming majority of representatives (73%) had school-age children, a prevalence far above that of the general public. Nearly half of House members—and 63% of representatives with current school-age children—sent their children to public schools. Put differently, a little over one-third of members with children selected private schools for them. Although a minority, this is well above the national average of 11% of students in private schools.[4] To the degree that these personal choices correlate with views about legislation, the lesser number of private school parents in the House, although above the national percentage, should have spelled support for the traditional public school system, albeit less than the general public's school choices would indicate.[5]

One might expect the choices parents make about their children's schools to be largely idiosyncratic. For example, religious attachments would be a consideration since many parochial schools have church ties. For members of Congress who are parents, factors such as personal

[3] The summary report, "How Members of Congress Practice School Choice," was accessed at http://www.heritage.org/library/backgrounder/bg1377.html in July 2000.

[4] Technically the percentages are not comparable since the units of analysis are different (parents versus children). Phi Delta Kappa/Gallup polls from 1999 to 2001 showed that 65% of adults had no children in school, 32% were public school parents, and 3% were private school parents.

[5] Unfortunately, I was unable to find a survey that asked respondents about their school choices that also included a congressional district identifier, so a full dyadic analysis like the one in the previous chapter is not possible. The General Social Survey (GSS) asked respondents in 1998 about the kinds of schools their children attended, but does not allow the respondents to be matched with House districts. The NES includes a district identifier but has not yet asked about private and public school choices.

wealth and decisions about whether their families will live primarily in the district or in Washington would be relevant. Even less predictable variables such as the social and educational needs of their children would enter into the calculations.

That these many variables are in play makes it all the more surprising that the school choice patterns of legislators are in fact systematically related to characteristics such as ideological preferences, suggesting that such choices are determined in part by their values. Interestingly, the ideological fault lines do not necessarily divide parents from those without children, or private versus public school parents. Rather, there is a clear distinction between private school parents in Congress and all other legislators. In terms of NOMINATE, representatives who chose public schools (.072) and representatives without children (.085) both looked moderate on average because they spanned party lines. In contrast, those who sent their children to private schools were decidedly right of center (.268). Private school parents in Congress were more likely to be Republican (65%) than either public school parents (49%) or legislators without school-age children (50%).

As a general indicator of voting support for traditional public education, I employ the National Education Association's (NEA) roll call score from the 1999 session of the 106th House. The NEA is the single largest labor union in the country and represents close to three million public school educators. The votes in the NEA scale deal with a variety of measures from specific items such as the Education Flexibility Partnership Act and the Teacher Empowerment Act but also more general items such as the Labor-HHS-Education appropriations bill and other spending bills, all of which are used to help the organization identify allies and enemies in its quest to support public schools. Figure 4.4 displays the distribution of scores (using a kernel density plot) separately for members with children in public school and members with children in private school. The figure is illuminating in two ways. First, both distributions are strongly bimodal, corresponding tightly to the strong partisan cleavage in the House.[6] This reflects the strategy adopted by the NEA and other interest groups of using vote ratings to separate enemies and allies (Fowler 1982; Snyder 1992). It also reflects the more general tendency of roll call votes to reveal two ideological voting blocs (Poole and Rosenthal 1997). Much like the scatterplot of district and legislator ideology in chapter 2 (figure 2.1), this graph suggests a strong role for partisanship and ideology as intermediate factors governing the translation of personal choices into public action.

[6] The distribution of NEA scores for members without school age children (not shown) is also bimodal and lies almost perfectly midway between the public and private distributions.

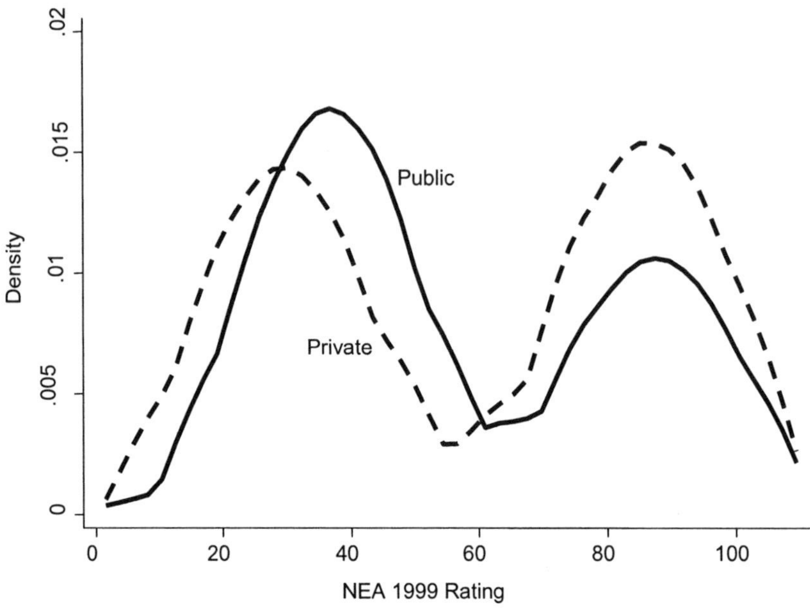

Figure 4.4. NEA scores of public and private school parents (1999)

Second, and more important here, is that parents of public school children vote more often with the NEA than do parents of private school children. Even with strong bimodality, public school parents' average scores are about 10 points more supportive of traditional public education. Although this difference needs to be confirmed in a full multivariate context, the figure at least makes plausible my hypothesis that personal traits affect legislative behavior, even at the crudest levels of aggregate roll call voting.

In building a regression model of legislative behavior, I repeat the approach used in the analysis of tobacco policy in chapter 3. I again test the connections in figure 2.2 between information, values, and self-interest and legislative action while controlling for lobbying influence by constituents and other interested participants. I use the school choices of representatives as proxies for information, values, and self-interest. Using just this indicator surely understates the role of personal factors since representatives' own experiences are much richer and more complex. All legislators have backgrounds as students themselves and many were also teachers or school administrators or have family and friends who work in school systems. As but one rough measure of personal roots, the decision to send one's children to public or private school probably reflects many of these other experiences.

I start with reactive measures of roll call voting behavior. As in the tobacco case, I analyze votes in the NEA scale already described and a specific roll call vote. The specific vote was taken on the Student Results Act, a measure offered by Richard Armey (R-TX) as an amendment to a larger education bill. Armey's House Amendment 536 would have established a pilot program to provide children who attend unsafe public schools $3,500 scholarships to attend different private schools chosen by their parents. The amendment failed 166–257–10 with most Democrats and 52 Republicans voting nay. Although taken on a modest program, the vote is useful because it provides for a direct measure of legislators' positions on a specific school choice proposal. Because the Armey amendment vote was also included in the original NEA index, I subtract it out to avoid analyzing the same dependent variable twice. The NEA rating is rescaled on the 0 to 100 range based on the remaining roll calls.

I estimate a logit model to identify the factors leading representatives to vote for or against the Armey amendment. My main interest is in how, controlling for other variables, representatives' choices about their children's schooling affect votes on the amendment. Because these variables mimic those used in the previous chapter, I move through the descriptions somewhat quickly here.

Partisan and ideological considerations should loom large in the analysis, as the bimodality in figure 4.4 hinted. Not only are NEA scores strongly polarized, but the amendment's sponsor was also the House majority leader, which should have sent strong cues to rank-and-file members of both parties. One might suspect that intense polarization will decrease the ability of background traits to explain variance in voting. In the analysis, party is measured as a dummy variable but as before is not included in the initial models. Instead I account for ideology using 1998 W-NOMINATE scores. As in earlier analyses, including both party and ideology in a single model is not permitted. They are highly correlated, and I believe that NOMINATE already measures partisanship to a significant degree. For now I include ideology along with other explanatory variables and later allow the effects of school choices to interact with party. This approach mimics the previous chapter's practice of running the models separately for Democrats and Republicans.

To factor in possible lobbying by constituents, I include three district characteristics that could influence members' thinking about reelection. As general indicators of support for public education, I include the percentage of college graduates in the district and the percentage of families with school-age children. As a measure of district ideology, Clinton's 1996 vote share in the district is used. A dummy variable for the South might be considered a measure of district preferences or culture as well. As before I include the legislator's race and sex to capture general policy predispositions highlighted in the literature. Because the lion's share of private elementary and secondary schools are Catholic, I include a dummy variable for representatives who identify as Roman Catholics. Finally, I include membership on the Education and Workforce Committee as a dummy variable in the event that members with peculiar education interests were overrepresented on that panel.

To be clear about expectations, I hypothesize that private school parents are more likely to support the Armey amendment, all else constant, while public school parents are more likely to oppose it. These school choices reflect their values and experiences, but they also shape those same values, providing new experiences and firsthand information about how well particular kinds of schools serve their children. Although the Armey plan was merely a pilot program, it was perceived as a step down the slippery slope of policy change away from the status quo. The NEA and other public school advocates opposed it as a threat to the existing system; proponents of private school choice may have viewed the program as overly modest but supported it as a way to demonstrate the potential of vouchers.

The first model appears in table 4.1, using linear regression to explain members' NEA voting scores (minus the Armey vote). Although the list of control variables is long, our main interest is in the effects of being a private or public school parent. Starting with the other variables, many of the usual suspects turn up as statistically significant predictors. Ideology of the district and the ideological voting patterns of the member are both highly significant and in the expected directions. A positive shift of .10 on the NOMINATE scale lowers one's NEA rating by about four points, while shifting the district 10 points in the conservative direction (i.e., lowering the Clinton vote share by .10) raises the NEA rating about two points. Other district indicators such as being in the South and having a higher number of couples with children are both associated with more support for the NEA's positions. Being a member of the Education Committee, at least during this period of Republican control, is associated with less support, and black members of Congress are less likely to vote with the NEA once ideology and other factors are considered.

More centrally, the school choice dummy variables suggest that personal decisions about children and schools do not affect general voting patterns on education issues. The coefficients for public and private school parents are far from statistically significant, indicating that school choices had no bearing on education votes once other factors such as ideology are considered. These null results are not especially surprising in light of the theory offered here. Legislators' traits do not uniformly affect their behavior. First, school choices of parent legislators ought to be highly conditional. Those opposing the status quo ought to be more sensitive to per-

TABLE 4.1
NEA Scale Votes

Public School Parent	2.17
	(2.10)
Private School Parent	1.04
	(2.36)
South	4.12*
	(1.98)
Public Ideology (W-NOMINATE)	−40.19**
	(2.05)
Couples with Children in District	.53**
	(.22)
Education in District	.01
	(.08)
District Ideology	22.26*
	(13.19)
Education & Workforce Committee	−7.60**
	(2.84)
Female	3.29
	(2.83)
Black	−16.52**
	(4.04)
Catholic	.24
	(2.13)
Constant	36.76**
	(11.88)
Number of Cases	365
Adjusted R^2	.69

Note: Cell entries are linear regression coefficients with standard errors in parentheses.

$^*p < .05$, $^{**} p < .01$, one-tailed test.

sonal traits than those pushing for change. Second, legislators' traits ought to become more consistent predictors of behavior once the level of analysis changes from the general to the specific. Although personal school choices do not influence the general index created by the NEA, they should be more prominent in votes on specific pieces of legislation having to do with private schools. The following analyses take up these two possibilities.

To evaluate whether public and private school choices are conditional on one's position toward the status quo, I create four new dummy variables that indicate a legislator's party affiliation and school choices. In this formulation it is assumed that Democrats tend to endorse the existing educational system with its emphasis on public schools while Republicans are more supportive of alternatives such as school choice and vouchers for private school tuition. The regression analysis is repeated substituting these four indicators. As table 4.2 shows, all four variables are highly significant predictors. But this does not necessarily demonstrate that school choices are conditional on partisanship. In fact, the coefficients for Democrats who send their children to private school and Democrats who send their children to public school are statistically indistinguishable. In addition, Republican legislators do not show sensitivity to the schools their children attend. The results merely show that, among parents of school-age children, Democrats' NEA scores are 11 points higher and Republicans are seven points lower than the median representative. The divide on general education matters is thus one of partisanship rather than personal choices. It is worth noting that few of the control variable effects change in important ways, except for district ideology, which drops out of statistical significance once legislator partisanship has been introduced to the model.

The differences between private and public school parents should become apparent as the dependent variable changes from an omnibus measure of public education support to specific votes that relate to private school choice. To test this possibility, I rerun the model, replacing the NEA scale with the vote on the Armey voucher amendment. Since the dependent variable is now dichotomous, the model employed is logit rather than ordinary least squares. The results in table 4.3 show support for a key prediction of the theory. The strong negative coefficient for the public school Democrat variable indicates that only Democratic legislators with children in public schools were significantly less likely to vote for the voucher program, after accounting for other influences. Republicans, who tend to support proposals such as Armey's, do not show much sensitivity to their personal school choices, but Democrats do. This is what one would expect if defenders of the traditional system of public education are most threatened by school choice proposals. Interestingly, no other variables aside from general ideological voting patterns (and being from the South) help explain votes on the Armey amendment. It would be unsettling if an ideology measure based on roll call votes did not continue to explain a roll call vote, especially on a polarizing issue such as school vouchers. It is more remarkable that Democratic public school

TABLE 4.2
Partisanship, School Choice, and NEA Scale Votes

Democrat: Public School Parent	10.88**
	(2.45)
Democrat: Private School Parent	10.81**
	(3.25)
Republican: Public School Parent	−6.60**
	(2.54)
Republican: Private School Parent	−6.83**
	(2.74)
South	3.01
	(1.87)
Public Ideology (W-NOMINATE)	−31.55**
	(2.33)
Couples with Children in District	.38*
	(.21)
Education in District	.04
	(.08)
District Ideology	12.86
	(12.31)
Education & Workforce Committee	−7.54**
	(2.62)
Female	5.47*
	(2.65)
Black	−13.10**
	(3.89)
Catholic	−.33
	(1.99)
Constant	42.73**
	(11.07)
Number of Cases	421
Adjusted R^2	.68

Note: Cell entries are linear regression coefficients with standard errors in parentheses.

$^*p < .05$, $^{**}p < .01$, one-tailed test.

TABLE 4.3
Armey Amendment Votes

Democrat: Public School Parent	−2.84** (1.18)
Democrat: Private School Parent	−1.54 (1.26)
Republican: Public School Parent	−.42 (.42)
Republican: Private School Parent	.31 (.48)
South	.74* (.41)
Public Ideology (W-NOMINATE)	4.33** (.63)
Couples with Children in District	.05 (.05)
Education in District	.03 (.02)
District Ideology	−4.27 (2.89)
Education & Workforce Committee	−.42 (.52)
Female	−.41 (.63)
Black	.52 (2.47)
Catholic	.65 (.46)
Constant	−2.80 (2.33)
Number of Cases	406
Log Likelihood	−110.73

Note: Cell entries are logit coefficients with standard errors in parentheses.

*$p < .05$, ** $p < .01$, one-tailed test.

parents distinguish themselves as opponents of the amendment even after controlling for ideology and other factors.

Although a shortage of data prevents extending the quantitative analysis to upstream activities such as sponsorship and speechmaking, the roll call voting models are informative in two respects. Legislators' actions on education policy are affected by their personal decisions about the kinds of schools their children attend. Even on a highly partisan vote, these background variables exert influence, which is a genuinely novel finding. Second, the pattern of effects differs depending on both partisanship and personal variables. Public school parents who are threatened by changes to the status quo are more likely to act out of introspective considerations. As defenders of the existing system, Democrats show a greater sensitivity to the public/private divide than do Republicans. It is now apparent that it would be misleading to conduct a standard analysis using an omnibus measure of roll call voting behavior. Personal factors do not appear until the researcher examines individual rather than aggregate indicators of legislative behavior.

Beyond these kinds of results, my theory further posits that personal factors and asymmetries are even more pronounced in shaping proactive behavior. In the case of the Armey amendment, most of these behaviors are unobservable because few speeches were given and the bill was brought to the floor so quickly that it lacked cosponsors. In the following section I turn to floor rhetoric to determine whether the small number of speeches made about vouchers refer to personal experiences. Although politicians make self-references for credibility or identification with constituents, I have set aside obvious campaign-style rhetoric to identify what appears to be more genuine personal reflection. Such mentions on the floor are a difficult test of the theory since much behavior is motivated by factors that a legislator does not mention publicly. Even Hall's (1996) heroic efforts noted that much of the "cloakroom" activity such as interpersonal lobbying cannot be documented in a systematic way. However, as he contends, observing briefly what occurs on the surface indicates deeper activity that remains out of view.

Framing on the Floor

The House debate over Armey's voucher proposal is notable for the heavy personalization of the arguments, this despite the general polarization around the issue at the time. Unlike many other issues, however, every legislator has some experience with schools. All were obviously students at one time, and most have advanced degrees. Many were also school administrators or teachers. A large number of members have children or grandchildren in school and gather information indirectly from them. Framing of education policy on the floor is fascinating because it highlights that members of Congress are attuned to diverse sets of considerations. Some arguments are fiscal in nature, but most are not. Some focus on the desirability of choice in the marketplace, while others (on both sides of the voucher debate) are concerned about equality of opportunity.

The frames surrounding the Armey proposal tended to invoke the values of duty and notions of what is right to do based on personal experience. The packaging used by most voucher advocates had to do with supporting free choice in the marketplace and protection of children in unsafe environments, both of which resonated with their overwhelmingly conservative ideologies. Defenders of the existing system cast vouchers as a challenge to the separation of church and state, thus privileging constitutional concerns over the value of personal autonomy in the marketplace. This view also fits comfortably within a liberal philosophy valuing public institutions.

Majority Leader Dick Armey (R-TX) initiated the discussion by pitching his voucher proposal in terms of the responsibility to serve the next generation. Much in the way that balancing the budget or protecting Social Security is framed as a duty, Armey presented the voucher option as the obligation of adults to children who lack opportunity. Armey motivated the proposal this way for his House colleagues.

> I have dealt with education all of my life, as a student, as a parent, as a teacher, and now as a grandparent and a legislator. One of the things that I have felt very seriously about in the last few days as I have thought about this bill is that all of a sudden, now as a grandparent, Mr. Chairman, I realize that these children for whom we talk about education today, my grandchildren, are more precious, or seem to be more precious to me at this time in my life, even than my own were at that time. Maybe that is just the business of being a grandparent. (October 21, 1999, H10623)

Representative Tom Tancredo (R-CO), a conservative and a former schoolteacher, amplified this point. But he also saw choice of schools much like other life choices, as a natural right not to be impeded by government. He brushed away Democratic concerns in this way.

> It is peculiar to say in the least that we get so concerned about this. It is not every child. We are not closing every school. My kid went to public schools. I taught in public schools. My wife just retired from a public school after 27 years. It is not that I have anything against public schools. I believe in them. . . . But what we must do is give people the ability to choose among them and between them. To take that away from human beings is taking away an absolute right. It is an admission of something that we must all do. (H10625)

In a debate about values, this sense of duty carries a lot of weight. Tancredo is asking Democrats in particular to overlook their biases and support the Armey proposal for the sake of marketplace choices that have the potential to help disadvantaged children.

In an interesting twist, Armey explained that the ways in which the membership of Congress differs descriptively from the public does a disservice to students who need safe schools.

> If my child or grandchild came home from school and had been a victim of assault on the school grounds and was injured . . . I would be able to pick up my child, my son would be able to pick up my grandchild and move him out of that school, get him someplace else, get him safe. A lot of families cannot do that. (H10624)

Congressman John Boehner (R-OH) held the same view. "Most of us in this Chamber are pretty fortunate. Our kids go to good schools. I know that my kid went to good public schools in my district; and, frankly, the schools in my district, by and large, are very good schools" (H10624). By emphasizing the privileges enjoyed by members, Boehner made the necessity of providing fair options to others through vouchers seem all the more compelling.

James DeMint (R-SC) seconded these arguments with an emphasis on his own children's self-interest. "I stand here today as a father and a businessman to explain why I believe this amendment is a reasonable and necessary one to secure the future for every American child by giving them an excellent education." He continued by stating the obvious but in personal terms. "As a father, I want my children to go to a school in a safe, orderly learning environment. I want them to be in a school which offers academic excellence" (H10624). There were plenty of members with educational backgrounds who backed Armey. One was Representative Jack Quinn (R-NY), a former public school teacher.

> I know the background of the gentleman from Pennsylvania [Education Committee chairman William Goodling] is in education. I happened to have been a middle school teacher for ten years before I came to work here in the Congress and know that there are some problems we will never fix no matter how much money we throw at them or throw toward them or with them. (H10638)

I have shown that choices about one's children's schools were a factor in determining not just positions but also activity levels. An occupational background in the education field does not necessarily make a member support or oppose school choice, but it is likely to translate into proactivity once preferences about education policy have been formed.

Religion can have the same mobilizing effect because so many private schools are parochial. Indeed, the vast majority are Roman Catholic. We might expect Catholic members of Congress to become sufficiently active on the issue to give a speech, even if the quantitative analysis showed that they voted no differently (at least once their children's school choices were controlled for). Of course, many Catholics who support vouchers will not make references to their religion or upbringing. Representative Boehner (R-OH) is one of those members: a Catholic school product and ardent advocate of choice who never made mention of his religion despite giving several floor speeches.

But for every few Boehners there is a member who allows his religion to become an explicit part of the evidence. A Notre Dame graduate and proud Catholic, Mark Souder (R-IN) argued that the contributions of Catholic schools ought to be supported by government programs. Parents, he pointed out, sacrifice to pay private school tuition and would benefit from federal assistance.

> The fact is in Cleveland, when the court just threw out their private school support program, the parents worked together to come up with that money because they are very concerned about the quality of education for their students. The Catholic Church for years has subsidized members of their parish who cannot afford it. . . . There are supplemental ways to get the income in. Some sacrifice for the parents. They are voting with their feet, and not every school costs like St. Albans, where our vice president may send his children or like the private schools in Washington where Members of Congress may send their children or the private schools around the country where the affluent send their children. There are many lower cost private schools where people, apparently the only people who can have those choices are middle-class and upper-class parents, not the lower-income people who need the desperate education.

Souder closed by noting his own public school roots, promising that even a full-scale voucher program would not harm public schools. If anything, the value of competition is that it would improve the public schools whose administrators fear losing their educational monopolies.

> I went to public schools; my kids are in public schools. Most people are not going to abandon their local school. It is close. They know the teachers. They are invested in it. But denying those who have the most at stake, who most need the best education possible, the possibility of even having a pilot program that would have to clear state legislature and a governor and give them an opportunity that if they can find a place where they can take this voucher or at least have the leverage to go to the school and say, "I might take my child out if you do not respond to some of my concerns," to deprive the powerless of any power over their school systems, they often have very little control over the school boards already. (H10642)

Other representatives described cases where students settled for less desirable public schools because private school tuition was unaffordable. "I can speak on this issue from personal experience," began Dave Weldon (R-FL). He presented his own story as an example of the working families who would be assisted with vouchers. "I can also speak that my father was a graduate of Catholic schools, and my sister went to Catholic school as well. My parents actually wanted to send myself and my two sisters, younger sisters, to Catholic school, but like so many working class families, they could not afford it."

As Souder had done, several speakers tried to dispel the feelings of threat to the existing educational structure by defending public schools while pushing for the pilot program. This is a wise rhetorical move given my theory of asymmetric participation. Boehner echoed Armey's appeal to duty, yet promised that the initiative would not undermine the status quo, but actually improve upon it.

Finally, it is worth pointing out that members can draw upon several different personal experiences even on a single bill. Representative Bob Etheridge (D-NC), who was North Carolina's superintendent of schools for eight years, pointed to several ways in which he had learned about public schools both directly and indirectly via family.

> When we start talking about children, it becomes very personal, as it should. With our three, they are fortunate. I wish all children had the opportunity to have those resources. Two of our children are engaged in public education. Our son is a fourth grade teacher in Wake County and listening to him talk about what happens in the classroom and this learning experience and how children need this help, and our daughter taught high school and is now back at the university. My wife is still in the public schools. Even though I left the superintendent's office, I did not get away from it. I get a dose of it every weekend I go home, but it is so important that we reach out and give children every opportunity. (April 4, 2000, H10745)

As Etheridge's appeal makes clear, the public debate often has personal roots. In the case of education policy, I have shown quantitatively that members' choices about the kinds of schools their children attend affect their votes. Floor rhetoric also points to a great deal of personalization. Although some personal references are used to help make a point more dramatic, most of them appear genuine. Shepherding a child through the school system or being a teacher or administer provides vivid, concrete, and lasting experiences. These experiences inform legislators' values, provide expertise, and focus self-interest, all of which may then affect reactive and especially proactive behavior on Capitol Hill.

Unfortunately, the analysis of proactive behavior on education policy must stop here. Data limitations preclude the more extensive kind of analysis conducted in the previous chapter. The small number of members who sponsored or gave speeches does not provide enough empirical leverage to make a multivariate analysis appropriate. As the next section shows, however, it is possible to detect consequences of personal values on factors other than roll call votes.

Consequences

Thus far this chapter has shown that members do indeed "shirk" when it comes to education policy. The analysis demonstrates not only that legislators fail to follow all of their constituents' views but also identifies precisely the factors that lead to policy discretion. Voters' ideological preferences are powerful determinants of education votes to be sure, but so too are representatives' personal experiences. To the degree that a legislator's school choices conflict with those of her constituents, pure policy representation can be distorted. This is not necessarily to make a negative judgment of "introspective representation" but to acknowledge that it happens. We have seen that parents of school-age children are far overrepresented in the House, and that the rate of private school attendance among these legislators' children is about three times that of the children of the general public. This skew in descriptive representation has consequences for the kinds of education policies that emerge from the House of Representatives.

As with tobacco, I expect there to be other consequences as well. Interest groups and campaign contributors are adept at identifying their enemies and allies in Congress. Groups' ratings, such as the NEA scale used in this chapter, are one means of distinguishing legislators based on roll call votes. PACs should be more likely to fund allies with supportive voting records than enemies who tend to vote against their interests. Moreover, I contend that groups become aware of the personal traits of members that are relevant to their concerns. In the case of education, I expect that teachers' unions learn about members' school choices and make campaign contributions at least partly in response to these personal choices.

I examine this possibility by modeling the total amount given to each incumbent by the NEA and American Federation of Teachers (AFT), the two dominant groups, representing roughly four million public educators. These PAC data come from the Center for Responsive Politics reports on the 2000 election cycle. These two PACs are no minor players in campaign finance; the CRP web site ranks the NEA as the third biggest donor of all time and the AFT as the fourteenth.[7] Moe (2003) illustrates the importance of the NEA in education policymaking, arguing that their electoral strategies are especially good at preventing change to the status

[7] The Center for Responsive Politics web site, www.opensecrets.org, records total donations made between 1989 and 2003.

Table 4.4
Determinants of NEA and AFT PAC Contributions to House Incumbents

Democrat: Public School	4373.72** (1008.63)	2982.89** (959.41)
Democrat: Private School	2604.07* (1322.85)	1217.45 (1248.24)
Republican: Public School	−4162.49** (1430.80)	−2295.05 (1414.65)
Republican: Private School	−6008.26** (1749.82)	−4235.43* (1723.79)
From South	−381.73 (932.33)	−1158.77 (902.92)
Public Ideology	−8497.46** (1138.83)	−3801.00** (1239.47)
NEA Voting Score	—	157.30** (22.36)
Couples with Children in District	111.09 (97.97)	50.98 (92.98)
Education in District	31.97 (38.07)	28.93 (36.08)
District Ideology	−1099.04 (5701.20)	−3183.40 (5420.46)
Education & Workforce	2424.01* (1222.19)	3917.43** (1172.18)
Female	202.75 (1175.76)	−637.70 (1109.26)
Black	−1637.26 (1709.10)	519.24 (1638.73)
Catholic	−307.85 (907.34)	−172.78 (858.35)
Constant	−2078.30 (5221.45)	−9302.22 (5080.82)
σ	6619.98** (333.780)	6176.91** (307.71)
Number of Cases	421	421
Log Likelihood	−2300.384	−2275.41

Note: Cell entries are one-sided tobit coefficients with standard errors in parentheses.
$^{*}p < .05$, $^{**}p < .01$, one-tailed test.

quo. Whether these massive interventions work or not, I wish to show that the education lobby's tactics are indeed sensitive to the personal backgrounds of the legislators they support or oppose.

Results of the PAC analysis appear in table 4.4. As before, the model is a one-sided tobit analysis of total contributions received. In these regressions I continue to control for the explanatory variables employed earlier. In the second column I add the NEA voting score in the event that teachers' groups are especially sensitive to their own ratings of legislators. (Note that NOMINATE and the NEA score are correlated at .74.) Of most interest in the table are the effects of partisanship and personal school choices.

The first model indicates a clear pattern of contributions that depend on both party affiliation (the major institutional cleavage) and personal school choices that legislators make for their children (a key personal factor). PAC donations are $4,374 more for Democrats who send their children to public school and $6,008 less for Republicans who send their children to private school. As we might expect in the contemporary Congress, the gap between parties (roughly $8,000) is greater than the difference between public and private school parents (roughly $2,000), but both matter independently and as interactions. In addition to these effects, the NEA and AFT PACs are more likely to give to liberals and donate about $2,400 more to members who serve on the Education Committee.

Similar results appear when the NEA score is added in the second column. The role of ideology wanes when this highly correlated roll call measure is added to the model, but it nonetheless appears that public education lobbies are sensitive to both. Committee members now appear to get even more of a financial boost, earning $4,000 more in donations. The pattern of effects for the partisanship and school choice interactions remains the same, running from highest for Democratic parents of public school children to lowest for Republican parents of private school children, even though the middle two steps no longer reach statistical significance. It is still true in this saturated model that Democrats receive more support if their offspring go to public schools, while Republicans receive less when they opt for private schools for their children. Democrats with children in public schools get $3,000 from teachers' unions, while Republicans with kids in private schools get $4,200 less than other members.

Conclusion

Substantively this chapter has shown that the personal experiences legislators have with their children's school choices affect their roll call votes on education policies generally and on school voucher plans especially.

Representatives with children in public schools are likely to vote with the NEA and against voucher programs, even more than representatives with children in private schools vote the other way. Those most threatened by proposed changes to the status quo were Democrats who endorsed the existing system of public elementary and secondary education.

On the voucher bill vote, public school parents were distinguished from other legislators in their opposition. Although votes on the Armey voucher proposal fell strongly along party lines, the interaction of personal school choices and partisanship was evident. Despite proponents' attempts to lessen the perceived threat to the status quo, Democrats with children in the public schools were strongly opposed to private school vouchers, while other configurations of party and school choice showed little effect. Sponsorship and speechmaking data were not abundant enough to conduct quantitative analyses, but even these asymmetric effects suggest the greater differences that are likely to emerge upstream in the policy process.

Not only do these interactions affect roll call voting, but political action committees appear to be aware of legislators' parenting and school choices. In addition to ideological considerations and favoritism toward members of the Education Committee, Democrats with children in public school received more PAC money than other legislators, while Republicans with children in private school received substantially less. The Democrat-private and Republican-public combinations fell predictably between these end points. More generally, rhetoric on the House floor about the Armey plan showed evidence of personalization. As in other policy domains, members of Congress do shirk from their constituents' and party's preferred positions, relying on their own personal values and experience when deciding how to vote.

CHAPTER FIVE

Religion and Morality

THE LAST DECADE HAS SEEN AN EXPLOSION of issues on the national agenda that deal in some way or another with religion, morality, or bioethics. From stem cell research to cloning to late-term abortions, federal policymakers have been forced to deal with matters of religious faith. These issues are intriguing for the power to pit technology against morality, science against conscience, and partisanship against personal conviction (Mooney 1999). For some participants, the policy choices are consistent and easy: supporting life, promoting research, ensuring liberty. For others, cross-cutting values and information pull them in different directions simultaneously. As a result, personal views such as religion can become valuable guideposts to help legislators navigate this murky and sometimes novel terrain.

In this chapter I examine two domains where religion appears to have played a role in the actions taken by members. The first set of bills concerns protections for religious practices. Starting with the Religious Freedom Restoration Act of 1993, Congress spent roughly a decade proposing and passing legislation designed to defend religious practices. These measures highlighted competing values in American society, particularly the debate between constitutional protection of religious practices and free speech versus government protection of the general welfare and the prohibition on the establishment of government-sponsored religion. As such, these initiatives were nothing less than a reexamination of the separation of church and state. The movement in the Clinton years to encode further protection of religious practices eventually morphed into George W. Bush's proposals to support "faith-based" organizations in the 2000 presidential election campaign. My analysis of this first domain concludes with a study of the Bush administration's proposal to provide some religious charities with public funding.

The second domain is the thicket of bioethical issues including cloning, stem cell research, euthanasia, and abortion. Although abortion has been a matter of partisan debate for several decades (Sanbonmatsu 2002a), the others matters are novel to many policymakers. In additional to pressure from Christian fundamentalist elements within the Republican Party, technological developments forced the Congress to face these issues as medical advances pressed onward through the 1990s. By 2001 President

Bush felt obligated to issue an executive order limiting federal funding of embryonic stem cell research; that same year Congress went on record for the first time on both stem cells and cloning. In this chapter I analyze action on the Human Cloning Prohibition Act of 2001 and demonstrate the influence of religious values on legislators' reactive and proactive responses to the bill.

Most of these legislative efforts—bans on cloning, new support for religious practices, and federal incentives to jump-start religious charities—were attempts to reverse the perceived trend toward secularization. In the 1990s a continual parade of news events about medical advances and other policy changes also hinted at the disappearance of absolute ethical standards about traditional human life. These included the 1997 announcement by Scottish scientists that cloning had produced Dolly the sheep, the 1993 Hawaii Supreme Court ruling in defense of same-sex marriage, followed by a 2000 civil unions law in Vermont, the 1998 airing of Dr. Jack Kevorkian's assisted suicide on the television program *60 Minutes,* and the 2001 announcement by a Massachusetts company that it had created the first cloned human embryo following the isolation of embryonic stem cells at the University of Wisconsin three years earlier. Religious conservatives felt threatened by the cloning experiments and bioethical slipperiness that appeared to ramp up in the 1990s and sought ways to hold onto traditional religious values. For many legislators their religious attachments are always near the surface, animating many of their policy views, but for others they reside more quietly under a professional veneer. I expect that religion is more important for those threatened by the new technological morality and for those who become proactive on these issues.

As one crude indicator of the threat posed by the secularization of society, figure 5.1 shows the changing religious attachments of Americans. The lines reflect the percentages of the adult public identifying roughly as Protestant, Catholic, or nonreligious in the NES.[1] What the figure shows is that the dominance of Protestants has fallen noticeably over the last 40 years, from more than three-quarters of the sample to just over half. Although Catholics increased their numbers, the largest increase is the rise of the nonreligious. The "Other/None" category in figure 5.1 grows more than tenfold. Although the United States remains one of the most religious nations, secularism has been also called the fastest-growing religion in modern America. This mirrors the rise in secularism and decline in church attendance documented by others (Norris and Inglehart 2004; Putnam 2000). This clear shift from traditional religiosity to more indi-

[1] For this figure only, Jews and other small non-Christian religions are omitted. The Other/None category include atheists, agnostics, humanists, and those reporting no religion.

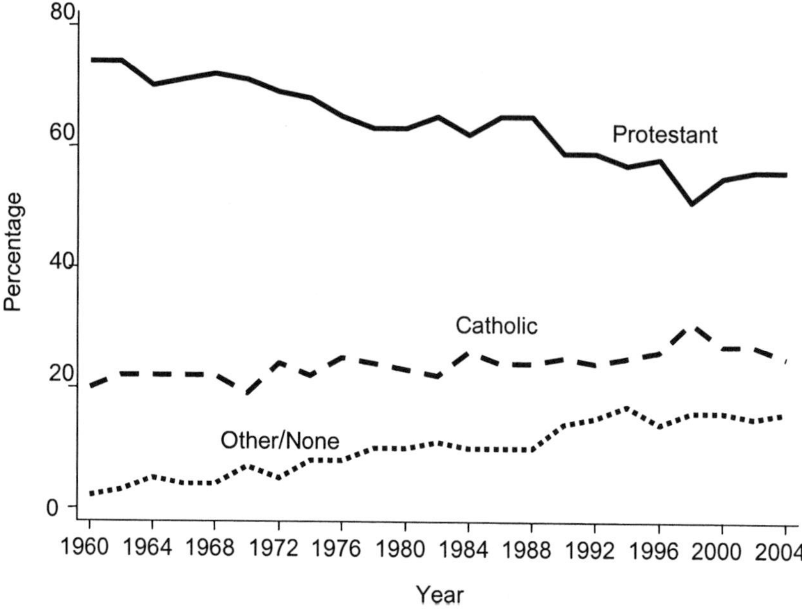

Figure 5.1. Adherence to major religious groupings (1960–2004). *Source:* National Election Studies.

vidualistic and secular orientations has not been lost on conservative Christians, who countered with new organizations and activism in the 1980s (Green, Rozell, and Wilcox 2003). Campbell (2006) has shown that evangelical Christians in particular respond to the rising threat of secular society by voting Republican more often in recent presidential elections. These sorts of challenges to previous understandings about family structure and human life more generally certainly threatened those who preferred the status quo to liberalization and might have contributed to the "culture wars" of the last 15 years.

In the remainder of this chapter I take up religious freedom, faith-based initiatives, and stem cell research. In each case I analyze how personal religious views affect legislative behavior qualitatively through floor speeches and quantitatively through statistical analysis of votes, sponsorship, and speeches. In contrast to earlier chapters, I focus on specific bills in every case. Although I cannot demonstrate the consequences of religious attachments on campaign contributions because of the legal status of most religious groups, the collection of three applications in a single issue domain makes a compelling case that religion is an important determinant of legislative behavior in the ways that my theory predicts. As crude an indicator as religious affiliation is, it nonetheless shows itself to be related to legislative action in predictable and important ways.

Data on Religions

In all three cases in this chapter the main variable of interest is the representative's religious affiliation. I categorize members as belonging to one of several religious families or traditions. This number of categories is more differentiated than those in figure 5.1 but does not require acknowledgment of every possible faith to which a member might belong. This family approach is common in the literature on religion and politics (Green et al. 1996). It allows for important distinctions in beliefs across religious traditions without expanding the number of categories to the point where no generalizations can be drawn.

In addition to these denominational categories, it would be useful to measure devotion, or the degree to which a person is committed to his faith. A person who merely identifies with a church is different from one who actively practices her religion. Unfortunately, this more nuanced way of assessing religion's role is not possible with my data, although anecdotes about Rick Santorum's deep Catholicism and other examples suggest that devotion does interact with denomination in important ways. My denominational approach almost surely understates the total impact of religion on policymaking and should be treated, like the other analyses in this book, as a first demonstration of the theory's potential.

Although not all coding systems are identical, my categories line up with existing approaches. The categories are Roman Catholic, White Evangelical Protestant, White Mainline Protestant, Jewish, Mormon, Black Protestant, and Other. These categories are mostly self-explanatory and follow existing coding systems. For example, white evangelicals include Southern Baptist, Pentecostal, Nazarene, Church of Christ, and others who belong to "hot" Protestant denominations with a more conservative interpretation of the Bible and adherence to universal standards. Mainline Protestant denominations are "cold" churches such as the Lutheran (ELCA), Presbyterian, and Methodist with moderate and more heterogeneous theological views. Black Protestants are African-American members who belong to historically black Protestant churches, most of them associated with the Methodist church in some form. The Other or Unaffiliated category includes unaffiliated members as well as those belonging to small denominations that are not easily classified as evangelical or mainline.

Across several House bills I record members' reactive and proactive legislative behaviors, namely roll call voting, cosponsorship, and speechmaking. In each case I examine how religious attachments affect these behaviors under the hypothesis that they should be more consequential for those defending the status quo and for proactivity compared to reactivity. Wherever data are available, I frequently confirm these expected asymmetrical effects.

I begin in table 5.1 by cross-tabulating the denominational attachments of members and their constituents in the 107th House of Representatives. As before, the distribution of religions in Congress is slightly distorted by the NES sampling procedure. The table represents the dyadic and collective representation of descriptive religious categories as seen from the constituent's point of view.

Starting with the collective representation perspective, we see that the column and row totals are often close but do not coincide precisely. Catholics are descriptively represented almost exactly as their population totals would suggest. Nearly a third of the public identified as Catholic in the 2000 NES, and the House proportion is similar.[2] The most overrepresented groups in terms of raw percentage differences are white mainline Protestants. Their strong presence appears to come at the expense of white evangelicals, who are surprisingly underrepresented at a rate of more than two to one. The smallest denominational families—black Protestants, Mormons, and Jews, are all overrepresented. Although the percentage differences between the House and population incidences are small, the ratios are quite large. For example, Jewish constituents are overrepresented at a rate of two to one.

More important for my argument are the discordant relationships at the dyadic level. Even if aggregate descriptive representation were perfect, many constituents would still be represented by legislators from different religious denominations. There is naturally some association between the representative's denomination and the constituent's denomination that occurs by shared values with voters or related criteria, but it is weak. Assuming independence between the two variables, by chance alone 25% of the respondents in table 5.1 would fall into concordant cells along the main diagonal if the two variables were distributed independently. The actual percentage of cases falling into congruent cells is only slightly higher at 33%, which suggests a lot of mismatches. Most evangelicals are represented by either mainline Protestant or Catholic members of Congress. Mainline Protestants are almost as likely to be represented by a Catholic legislator as one from their own religious family. If we collapse categories further, about a quarter of white Protestants are represented by

[2] Although the table shows Catholicism to be more common in the House than in the population, the table does not accurately represent the House as noted in previous chapters. The actual percentage in the House is close to 29% compared to 32% in the NES sample.

TABLE 5.1

Collective and Dyadic Representation of Religious Denominations

		Constituent Denomination							
		Catholic	*Jewish*	*Mormon*	*White Evangelical*	*White Mainline*	*Black Protestant*	*Other*	*Total*
Representative Denomination	Catholic	220 (45.6%)	13 (37.2%)	*	99 (21.0%)	168 (27.6%)	*	10 (22.7%)	515 (33.8%)
	Jewish	23 (4.7%)	11 (32.7%)	*	14 (2.9%)	12 (2.7%)	*	*	65 (4.3%)
	Mormon	20 (4.1%)	*	22 (63.8%)	9 (1.9%)	16 (3.7%)	*	6 (12.4%)	74 (4.8%)
	White Evangelical	44 (9.1%)	*	*	81 (17.2%)	71 (15.9%)	*	*	201 (13.3)
	White Mainline	138 (28.7%)	*	6 (18.0%)	202 (43.0%)	162 (36.4%)	*	19 (42.3%)	537 (35.3%)
	Black Protestant	18 (3.7%)	*	*	59 (12.6%)	8 (1.8%)	*	*	91 (6.0%)
	Other	20 (4.2%)	*	*	6 (1.3%)	9 (1.9%)	*	*	38 (2.5%)
	Total	482 (31.7%)	35 (2.3%)	34 (2.2%)	471 (31.0%)	446 (29.3%)	9 (0.6%)	45 (0.3%)	1,521

Source: 2000 National Election Study and author coding of 107th House of Representatives.

* indicates five or fewer cases in a cell.

Catholics; almost 40% of Catholics are represented by Protestants. Disaggregation of religious families would reveal even more discordant relationships. Shirking has as much potential in this setting as any.

For these discordant relationships to be worth studying, denominational affiliations must have some bearing on congressional behavior. A voter who chooses a "type" of legislator based in part on religious identity might be doing so rationally if personal faith affects public action. I show this to be true in three different settings.

The Religious Freedom Restoration Act of 1993

My first case represents one episode in the ongoing debate over religious freedoms. Congress and the Supreme Court have batted issues of religious liberties back and forth for over a decade. In an opening salvo, in 1990 the Supreme Court ruled in *Employment Division v. Smith* that religious practices could be curtailed by laws designed to maintain public order. The case concerned two Native Americans who were fired by their employer for smoking peyote as part of a religious ceremony. The Court held that the defendants' First Amendment rights were trumped by state drug laws and suggested that other religious expressions could be illegal as long as laws were not designed to target particular practices. The *Smith* decision turned out to be only the first act in a series of tit-for-tat exchanges between Congress and the courts that would redefine religious freedom several times in the 1990s. In response to the decision, a Democratic Congress immediately moved to pass legislation that protected individual religious rights. The religious freedom bill introduced in the 102nd Congress quickly became tangled up in side debates about whether the legislation could be used to challenge abortion laws. Opposed by the Catholic Church and many pro-life legislators, the bill stalled.

In the next Congress Charles Schumer (D-NY) reintroduced H.R. 1308, also known as the Religious Freedom Restoration Act (RFRA). With new language excluding abortion as a protected religious practice, nearly every religious group supported the legislation, as did the American Civil Liberties Union (ACLU). As a result of this broad coalition, RFRA sped through the legislative process. Introduced on March 11, 1993, it was reported to the full House and brought to the floor just two months later. The bill was passed under suspension of the rules with a simple voice vote. Like other religious matters considered in this chapter, the bill brought together strange bedfellows Orrin Hatch (R-UT) and Edward Kennedy (D-MA), who are adherents of rather different religious denominations and are at opposite ends of the ideological spectrum. By the end of the year the Senate had also agreed to the bill 97–3, and President Clinton signed it into law in November.

The overwhelming support for the bill on the floor prohibits an analysis of roll call voting on RFRA, but other forms of member endorsement showed more variability. Despite the wide support for RFRA at the time of the vote, only 170 members of the House signed on as cosponsors. If most members were planning to vote for the bill, it is curious that less than a majority added their names in support of RFRA. Members were even more selective about speaking on the floor about the bill. Fewer than two dozen took to the floor to support RFRA, despite widespread public enthusiasm for the legislation. In this section I analyze the proactive decisions to cosponsor and speak about RFRA in the 103rd House of Representatives.

As an initial step, table 5.2 reports RFRA sponsorship rates by party and religious family. In addition to the greater tendency of Democrats than Republicans to sponsor RFRA, there are more substantial differences across denominational groupings. Only about a third of white Protestants in the House cosponsored RFRA, while nearly every Jewish member did so. Most interesting is the interaction of religion and partisanship. Almost 40% of mainline Protestants supported RFRA if they were Democrats; only about 20% did so if Republicans. The gaps are smaller for Catholic and evangelical members, but they exist nonetheless. Being Christian or Republican made one less likely to cosponsor RFRA; being both was an especially strong deterrent. As in the other applications in this book, the side a legislator was on appears to have interacted with his personal characteristics in predictable but also nonuniform ways.

To determine whether these conditional effects are genuine, I examine the sponsorship measure with multivariate analysis. As before, I first estimate the model for all representatives, then separately within parties. The independent variables once again include measures of legislator ideology (NOMINATE), district preferences (the Clinton vote share in 1992), and dummy variables for the South and the member's sex.[3] I also control for membership on the Judiciary Committee, which reported the bill, and general cosponsorship propensities of members. New here are dummies for each of the religious families.[4] Contrary to standard practice, I included all of these denominational dummies and omitted the constant. This allows me to avoid omitting one of the dummies, but does require the reader to compare the coefficients to one another rather than to the omitted category.

Table 5.3 reports logit results predicting whether a member sponsored RFRA. Following the approach adopted in the previous chapter, the analy-

[3] Race is omitted because it is highly collinear with the Black Protestant dummy variable.

[4] The smallest denominational groupings often do not provide enough variation or enough cases to include in multivariate analysis. As table 5.1 shows, there were only a few Democratic Mormons and Republican Black Protestants.

Table 5.2
Cosponsorship of RFRA, by Party and Religious Family

Religious Family	*Democrats*	*Republicans*
White Mainline Protestant	37.9% (87)	20.4% (93)
Catholic (and Orthodox)	33.3 (78)	18.6 (43)
White Evangelical Protestant	30.0 (20)	23.8 (21)
Black Protestant	61.8 (34)	100.0 (1)
Jewish	88.9 (27)	100.0 (5)
Other or Unaffiliated	80.0 (10)	100.0 (5)
Mormon	100.0 (2)	100.0 (7)
Total	46.5 (258)	28.9 (175)

Note: Religious families are listed in order by the number of members in each.

Cell entries are the percentage of members cosponsoring RFRA with the total number of cases in parentheses below.

sis is first conducted on the full set of legislators and then separately by party to identify conditional effects. Because the constant is omitted, each of the religious dummy coefficients is interpretable only relative to the others. Protestants of all stripes were less likely to cosponsor RFRA than were legislators from smaller denominational families. Catholics were perhaps less likely than Protestants to cosponsor, although the magnitude of the Catholic coefficient is not statistically larger than that for the three Protestant groups. Conservatives were also more likely to sponsor the bill, as were members who tend to cosponsor frequently.

Importantly, the effects of one's religious denomination appear to be unequal across the two parties. My theory contends that Republicans, who are more likely to be on the defensive in this domain, would be more likely to act on personal factors when making choices about whether to cosponsor RFRA. The coefficients on the Catholic and white Protestant variables are in fact larger in magnitude for Republicans than for Demo-

TABLE 5.3
Cosponsoring the Religious Freedom Restoration Act

Explanatory Variable	*All*	*Democrats*	*Republicans*
Catholic	−3.20**	−3.40**	−5.50**
	(.74)	(.87)	(1.44)
Jewish	−.37	−.64	−2.23
	(.88)	(1.01)	(1.87)
Mormon	−.10	—	−1.62
	(1.00)		(1.45)
White Evangelical Protestant	−2.54**	−2.74**	−4.24**
	(.74)	(.87)	(1.44)
White Mainline Protestant	−2.62**	−2.66**	−4.87**
	(.67)	(.78)	(1.29)
Black Protestant	−2.48*	−2.82*	—
	(1.05)	(1.21)	
Other Religion or Unaffiliated	.02	−1.74	—
	(1.05)	(1.15)	
Female	.23	.24	.08
	(.37)	(.43)	(.81)
From South	−.13	−.12	.19
	(.27)	(.35)	(.49)
District Ideology (Clinton %)	.02	.01	.08*
	(.02)	(.02)	(.03)
Public Ideology (NOMINATE)	−.88**	−2.26*	−2.14*
	(.33)	(.98)	(1.23)
Judiciary Committee	−.65	−.76	−.85
	(.47)	(.58)	(.91)
Total Cosponsorships	.004**	.004**	.005*
	(.001)	(.002)	(.002)
Number of Cases	423	254	169
Log Likelihood	−226.11	−142.43	−76.23

Note: Entries are logit coefficients with standard errors in parentheses. Empty cells indicate variables dropped due to insufficient cases or variation. Constant suppressed.

* $p < .05$, ** $p < .01$, one-tailed test.

crats. Republicans also appear more responsive to district ideology and Democrats more responsive to their own ideologies, but this difference may be artificial because of collinearity between the variables and greater variation in presidential vote measure among Republicans. None of the other control variables' effects varies between the parties.

Members from opposing parties differed in activity levels because they differed in denominational makeup. The Democrats' greater likelihood of sponsoring the bill is more a product of the differing religious compositions of the parties than of partisanship itself. Indeed, while many of the differences *across* religious families are statistically significant at conventional levels, only one—the higher rates of sponsorship among Democratic mainline Protestants—is significant *within* a family.

To reiterate, the effects of religion are also conditional on party affiliation, as was the case with personalistic variables analyzed in the previous two chapters. While the aggregate differences in sponsorship behavior between Democrats and Republicans were driven mostly by differing compositions of adherents within the parties, there is also evidence that Republicans translate their denominations into action more fervently.

Next I analyze floor speeches about RFRA. As noted above, this is an even more selective activity than is cosponsorship. The small number of speakers makes a party-specific analysis untenable, but it is possible to estimate a single model that includes all members to determine whether religious affiliation has a direct effect on floor speeches. Table 5.4 reports a logit model of the likelihood of giving a speech about RFRA on the floor using the same set of explanatory variables for all House members.

Not surprisingly, members of the referring committee were especially likely to speak since they were managing the floor debate and felt responsible for advocating for its passage. In contrast to cosponsoring, neither district ideology nor a member's public ideology is statistically significant. In their place, personal characteristics become more important. Women were more likely to speak about the bill. Religious denominations were important as well. Although not all of the denominational dummy variables are statistically different from one another, several are of rather different magnitudes. Black Protestants were especially unlikely to speak, while Mormons and white evangelicals were more likely to take part. Members from evangelical Christian denominations became overrepresented in the public debate, even after taking into account their general left-right voting records and the ideological positions of their constituents.

More generally, it appears that legislators from the smallest denominations were most likely to speak, as the slightly larger (i.e., less negative) coefficients suggest. Black Protestants aside, the largest groups (Catholics and mainline Protestants) showed the least initiative, while the smallest groups (evangelicals, Jews, Mormons, and others) were most proactive.

TABLE 5.4
Speeches about the Religious Freedom Restoration Act

Catholic	−6.00**
	(1.45)
Jewish	−5.37**
	(1.49)
Mormon	−3.48*
	(1.71)
White Evangelical Protestant	−4.58**
	(1.43)
White Mainline Protestant	−5.86**
	(1.32)
Black Protestant	−7.78**
	(2.16)
Other Religion or Unaffiliated	−4.98**
	(1.43)
Female	1.66*
	(.65)
From South	.06
	(.65)
District Ideology (Clinton %)	.04
	(.03)
Public Ideology (NOMINATE)	−.29
	(.69)
Judiciary Committee	2.94**
	(.62)
Number of Cases	423
Log Likelihood	−65.17

Note: Entries are logit coefficients with standard errors in parentheses. Constant suppressed.
* $p < .05$, ** $p < .01$, one-tailed test.

This result will be echoed in other analyses and is a pattern that fits with my expectations about the role of threat as a motivator. Presumably it is the smallest denominations that feel the most need to defend their religious liberties with legislation.

My analysis of action on RFRA sits well with the larger argument about members' backgrounds, proactive legislating, and asymmetries between the majority and the minority. I find that religious affiliations begin to have an influence at the cosponsorship stage. Cosponsorship is more proactive and selective than roll call voting. The choice to sign onto the bill was motivated in part by religious identity, although ideology and overall cosponsorship activity were predictive as well. Dividing the analysis by party suggested that religion mattered more for Republicans, as did district preferences. Although support for RFRA was widespread, the heightened influence of religion for Republicans is consistent with my theory because it was primarily Republicans who felt threatened by the Court's actions and thus wished to revert to the previous status quo. Although my analysis of floor speeches was more limited, religion appeared to play an even more central role there in motivating behavior. Ideology became a nonfactor at this highly selective stage, and another personal characteristic, sex, became a statistically significant predictor of action.

The Community Solutions Act of 2001

As the Clinton administration gave way to the second Bush administration in early 2001, politicians' views about the role of religion became markedly more salient in the policy process. George W. Bush emphasized his Christian faith and campaigned for the presidency in 2000 as a "compassionate conservative." The "compassion" stemmed in part from his own values, but also from a belief that government ought to encourage religious organizations to play a larger role in doing social good. He advocated "faith-based initiatives" to support religious charities and established a White House agency devoted to these initiatives.

To boost charitable giving to religious and other organizations, a new Charitable Choice policy was proposed that would allow taxpayers who do not itemize deductions on their income tax returns to begin getting credit for contributions to nonprofit religious organizations. The legislation also expanded government funding for religious groups that provide social services without restricting their religious activities. The idea had it roots in the massive welfare reforms of 1996, which for the first time allowed federal funds to be used by faith-based organizations. Charitable Choice was introduced in the House in early 2001 as H.R. 7. Its lead sponsor was Representative J. C. Watts (R-OK), who was not only one of the few black Republicans to ever serve in Congress but more importantly had been a Protestant minister before entering the House.

The bill initially appeared headed for quick passage. Despite losing the popular vote in 2000, President Bush was claiming a mandate for his policy proposals and had a firm Republican majority in Congress to support him. Senators Rick Santorum (R-PA) and Joseph Lieberman (D-CT) had been pushing a similar bill before Bush's election. Charitable Choice made its way through two House committees—Judiciary and Ways and Means—quickly and came to a floor vote in July. Along the way Watts's bill had also gathered 44 cosponsors. Although the bill stalled in the Senate over concerns about hiring discrimination, the final floor vote in the House was successful and fell almost perfectly along party lines, passing 233 to 198.

While a relatively close vote, the House roll call on Charitable Choice was not particularly interesting since only 19 members crossed party lines. Empirically, this high level of partisanship makes it impossible to estimate the roll call vote model by party. The power of partisanship at this final (and I would emphasize, most reactive) stage also stacks the deck against finding any effects of other variables.

Sponsorship provides better leverage on the proactive choices of members. In the case of H.R. 7, it represents an effort by about one of every 10 members to throw his clout behind the bill. Even though a (quite partisan) majority of the House supported the bill in the end, the selective tendencies of members of this majority to endorse the bill ahead of time are enlightening. It reminds us that while partisan concerns might dominate the most public and final roll call decisions made by members, other factors play a larger role upstream in the lawmaking process.

Floor speeches on Charitable Choice hint at the role that religious identities played in proactive legislating. A social justice advocate, Tony Hall (D-OH) had already shown great support for public funding of religious initiatives. Hall was a nondenominational Christian married to a Catholic, a former Peace Corps volunteer, and a supporter of religious philanthropy. As chair of the Select Committee on Hunger, in 1993 he fasted for 22 days to draw attention to hunger and his committee. Hall explained how easy it was for him to cross party lines to support President Bush on the issue.

> When the gentleman from Oklahoma [J. C. Watts] and the White House asked if I would be interested in sponsoring this faith-based initiative, I did not hesitate. It was not much of a stretch for me. It was, as some people have said, a no-brainer. I did not have to think too long or hard about it because I have had a lot of experience with faith-based programs and people of faith. I admire them and what they do.

Hall's perspective allowed him to see the value of religion in solving hunger and other crises. He experienced the power of faith at home and when he "traveled to East Timor and Indonesia and visited poverty alleviation projects." Hall was convinced in these visits that religious fervor motivates social good.

> I toured squalid neighborhoods in Jakarta where hundreds of thousands of people lived in dumps and in conditions not fit for humans. As I visited these

> projects where repugnant smells were everywhere and hunger and sickness were rampant, I asked the workers why they did this work that they did. I knew what they were going to say to me, because when I ask this question, whether I am in Indonesia, Dayton, Ohio, or rural Appalachia, I always get the same answer. They tell me what motivates them is their faith. (July 31, 2001, H4224)

Many lawmakers conceded that religious organizations do tremendous social good, but they expressed First Amendment fears about the government's endorsing them. One concern about government funding of religious programs is that those being served would be subject to proselytizing or even exclusion from services if they failed to endorse the religious group's views. Hall downplayed this worry, as did many Republicans. In response to Barney Frank's (D-MA) tale of a soup line that forbade non-Jews from participating, Joe Scarborough (R-FL) drew on personal experience to confront this criticism.

> But there is a culture, seriously, there is an inherent culture in these organizations, like, for instance, and I'll talk about my church. I'm Southern Baptist. I disagree with a lot of things they believe about people who are divorced not being able to be deacons or, or women not being able to preach, all right? But I do know that there are Southern, and if that offends me, I can, I can take a hike. But there are, even though I disagree with some of the things that people in the Southern Baptist Church believe in, they can effectively deliver services because of the culture. (H4224)

At this point Scarborough was interrupted by Carrie Meek (D-FL), who decried his statement as an "outrage." Meek explained, "I got religion in a lean-to many years ago, so there is very little my colleagues can tell me about faith based. But they can say to me that they want to discriminate, and I can hear that in whatever language they speak it in" (H4254). In accord with the RFRA findings about differently sized denominations, it again appears that members of the dominant religious families—Hall the Catholic and Scarborough the evangelical—are most supportive of faith-based initiatives, while members from small denominations—Frank a Jew and Meek a black Protestant—are most opposed.

In table 5.5 I model the vote on Charitable Choice. The explanatory variables are essentially the same used in the analysis of RFRA. I add a dummy for members of Ways and Means since the bill was referred to that committee as well as Judiciary. As might be expected given the extremely partisan nature of the vote, public ideology is the only significant predictor. (NOMINATE and party affiliation are correlated at greater than .90 in the 107th House.) If one adopted the standard approach of studying only roll call votes, the empirical probing would end here and the researcher would falsely conclude that Charitable Choice was the

TABLE 5.5
Determinants of Charitable Choice Vote

Catholic	.50 (1.52)
Jewish	−.53 (2.10)
Mormon	−.18 (2.73)
White Evangelical Protestant	1.99 (1.74)
White Mainline Protestant	.97 (1.59)
Other Religion or Unaffiliated	.77 (2.60)
Female	−1.16 (1.02)
From South	−.28 (.67)
District Ideology (Bush %)	−.02 (.03)
Public Ideology (NOMINATE)	7.55** (.87)
Judiciary Committee	−.01 (1.87)
Ways and Means Committee	−.06 (1.19)
Log Likelihood	−49.27
Number of Cases	430

Note: Entries are logistic regression with standard errors in parentheses. Constant suppressed. Black Protestant dummy variable omitted due to lack of variation.
* $p < .05$, ** $p < .01$, one-tailed test.

product of nothing but ideology and partisan concerns. Personal characteristics seemingly had no effect on how members reacted to Bush's faith-based initiatives proposal, beyond the degree to which they initially shaped party affiliations. While this unidimensional view of congressional politics might adequately describe aggregate, and especially passive behavior, my theory posits that it becomes less adequate as one moves upstream in the policymaking process.

To examine more proactive behavior earlier in the process, Table 5.6 takes the next step, repeating the analysis with cosponsorship of H.R. 7 as the dependent variable. As in other sponsorship models, a measure of total cosponsorship activity is added to control for baseline tendencies, but otherwise the model is the same except that a couple of small denominational categories have been removed because of insufficient variation. Public ideology still matters, but much less, as its coefficient drops

TABLE 5.6
Determinants of Charitable Choice Sponsorship

Catholic	1.99*
	(1.13)
White Evangelical Protestant	2.48*
	(1.13)
White Mainline Protestant	2.42*
	(1.12)
Female	−.41
	(.72)
South	−.07
	(.38)
District Ideology (Bush %)	.02
	(.03)
Public Ideology (NOMINATE)	2.86**
	(.69)
Judiciary Committee	1.22*
	(.54)
Ways and Means Committee	−.03
	(.60)
Total Cosponsorships	.007**
	(.002)
Constant	−8.49**
	(1.97)
Log Likelihood	110.10
Number of Cases	433

Note: Logistic regression with standard errors in parentheses. Constant suppressed.

* $p < .05$, ** $p < .01$, one-tailed test.

by more than half. Factors that failed to influence the roll call vote now emerge as statistically significant predictors. Curiously, district ideology remains unrelated to action on Charitable Choice, but members of Judiciary and legislators who tend to cosponsor frequently were more likely to cosponsor H.R. 7. The more compelling results have to do with religion. Compared to the excluded groups, Protestants, whether evangelical or mainline, are much more likely to sponsor the charitable choice initiative. Catholics, who were familiar with the gargantuan Catholic Charities, were also more likely to cosponsor the bill. These findings run contrary to the RFRA findings, in which small denominations were more likely to support the bill, but there the underlying mechanism was threat to religious liberty. With Charitable Choice the threat is less a concern than is the desire to codify practices that provide a tax break for donations contributed by the millions of Protestant and Catholic adherents nationwide.

Although the data are too thin to analyze sponsorship by party, recapping the overall results is informative. Simply put, religious attachments became increasingly important predictors of legislative behavior as the locus of study moved from roll call votes to bill sponsorship. Moving upstream in the legislative process privileges proactivity, and proactive behavior is more likely to be driven by personal experiences and interests than are roll calls taken at the end of the process. Although partisan cleavages dominated the final stage, personal factors helped shepherd the bill to the point of the vote.

Human Cloning Prohibition Act of 2001

A series of high-profile advances—primarily attempts at gene therapy and cloning—turned stem cell research from a quiet industry into a hot issue in the late 1990s. Scientists and doctors had quietly worked with adult stem cells for years before politicians took notice. For example, bone marrow transplants transfer adult stem cells from one person to another, yet seldom attracted controversy. These cells are also used to combat diseases such as leukemia and lymphoma on a daily basis. More controversial and even more promising are embryonic stem cells, which came into public awareness only recently. They are more flexible than adult stem cells and may be helpful in tackling such difficult conditions as Parkinson's disease, Alzheimer's disease, and diabetes.

Controversy arose because embryonic stem cells are harvested from a blastocyst: a sperm-egg combination that may eventually form a fetus. Harvesting the cells prevents the blastocyst from developing and thus prevents a potential birth from occurring. Those who oppose abortion also typically oppose the creation of new embryonic stem cell colonies under the reasoning that both procedures unnaturally end human life. Pressured in part by Christian fundamentalists within his party, President Bush was required to face this complex scientific and ethical issue soon after coming to office. After contemplating the issue himself and discussing it with others, Bush announced in August 2001 that federal funding would not support any embryonic stem cell research on new lines, a departure from the Clinton administration's policy. This decision was something of a compromise between the Republican antiabortion base and the more secular scientific community. Those endorsing a "culture of life" wished Bush had gone further. Scientists who depend on government funding were dismayed that they would not have access to more than a few dozen of the many thousands of stem cells already in existence. As a result, Bush's decision did more to thrust the issue further into the limelight than to resolve it.[5]

Stem cell research is a fascinating issue because it cuts across traditional political cleavages, both among the public and in Congress. Although Democrats were more likely than Republicans to support such research, members often crossed the partisan divide. Several pro-life Republicans joined Democrats in urging Bush to liberalize his ban on stem cell funding. Among them were all five Mormon senators, led by Orrin Hatch (R-UT). Chapters 1 and 2 noted several cases where personal experiences pushed members to become advocates of stem cell research, from Representative Diana DeGette's diabetic daughter to Senator Arlen Specter's cancer scares. Like so many other issues, the effects of these background experiences were often asymmetric. Likewise, we shall discover that religious affiliation's effect on support for stem cell research was more important for Republicans than Democrats. The Catholic Church and evangelical faiths such as the Southern Baptists were most clearly opposed to stem cell research of any type, although lay Catholics were much more supportive than was their church leadership. Officially the Episcopalians, Presbyterians, and Methodists all adopted nuanced positions that generally supported research, particularly on existing lines.

Public opinion became detectably more supportive of embryonic stem cell research, particularly after Bush's policy announcement in 2001 (Nisbet 2004). Public opinion surveys conducted by the Pew Center for the People and the Press showed an increase in those "valuing research" compared to those wanting to "protect embryos" from a 27–52 split in early 2002 to a 47–41 split in late 2004. Among the most supportive denominations were secularists (70–16), followed closely by Catholics and mainline white Protestants. Most opposed were white evangelicals and to some degree black Protestants.

[5] Five years later, in July 2006, the Congress would vote to extend federal funding for research on embryonic stem cells that were discarded from fertility clinics and other sites. President Bush issued his first veto to prevent the bill from becoming law.

Around the time President Bush announced his decision on federal funding for embryonic stem cell research, Congress moved to stop undesirable biomedical practices. In July 2001 the House voted to ban all cloning of embryos. As *CQ* noted, "It was the first time either chamber had gone on record on what was one of the most rapidly growing areas of the life sciences" and an issue "requiring lawmakers to consider whether days-old embryos deserve the same moral status as a person" (2001 *Almanac,* 16–3). Although few members would support full human cloning, some Democrats asked that the bill allow for therapeutic cloning of cells to combat disease. Similar legislation banning cloning appeared in 1997, but it was defeated by "some unlikely opponents: abortion foes, such as Strom Thurmond, R-S.C., and former Sen. Connie Mack, R-Fla. (1989–2001), argued that the bill was too broad, citing personal and family experiences with serious diseases" (16–3).

Politicians are trained to avoid highly charged issues such as religious views, yet congressional floor debate reveals many instances where members invoked their own religious views. Doctors also relied upon their medical expertise. Physician and senator Bill Frist (R-TN) drew on his experience in the operating room.

> I, indeed, am pro-life. I oppose abortion. My voting record on the floor of this body is consistent with that. Those beliefs are based on the very strongly held spiritual beliefs that I have. They are based on my medical understanding, having spent 20 years in the field of medicine, and in science—that medical understanding of this process of life and of living tissues. I do give moral significance to the embryo. (July 18, 2001, S7846)[6]

Another doctor, bill sponsor David Weldon (R-FL), gave the House a brief lecture on "somatic cell transfer" complete with visual aids. He explained that the cloning process interrupts an embryo's development.

> I studied embryology in medical school. I am a physician. I practiced medicine for 15 years. Indeed, I brought my medical school embryology textbook [to the floor today], and I would defy anybody in this body to tell me what the science behind making the assertion that this is not a human embryo. There is absolutely no basis in science to make such a claim. (July 31, 2001 H4907)

Yet being a physician does not dictate a particular position on the morality of embryonic stem cell research. Representative Jim McDermott (D-WA), a supporter of federal funding for such research, introduced his remarks this way:

> I wanted to come to the well tonight to talk a little bit about an issue that has gotten a lot of attention here on the floor, lots of talk and lots of rhetoric, and

[6] Frist would later modify this view to permit research on discarded embryos.

> that is the whole question of embryonic stem cell research. I am a physician and I know firsthand about taking care of these people; I know about health and the issues of morality, and I have devoted my life to trying to improve the health and well-being of individuals, both in the Congress and in the legislature, as well as in my office. (August 02, 2001, H5327)

Congressman Ron Paul (R-TX) is also a doctor, but his scientific interests, moral concerns, and libertarian values are in some conflict. "As an obstetrician gynecologist with 30 years of experience with strong pro-life convictions I find this debate regarding stem cell research and human cloning off-track, dangerous, and missing some very important points." Paul continued with a series of rhetorical questions.

> For instance, should a spontaneously aborted fetus, non-viable, not be used for stem cell research or organ transplant? Should a live fetus from an ectopic pregnancy removed and generally discarded not be used in research? How is a spontaneous abortion of an embryo or fetus different from an embryo conceived in a dish? (July 31, 2001 H4926)

If medical experience does not push a legislator in a particular direction, firsthand encounters with medical traumas usually do. It is hard to personalize the issue much more than Republican congressman Jim Ramstad (R-MN) did. He rose on July 17 to make the following statement.

> Della Mae is a wonderful, loving, 79-year-old woman totally debilitated by Alzheimer's disease. Joey was a promising young man in his early 20s who died a horrible death; a cruel, tragic death from diabetes. Mr. Speaker, Della Mae is my mother. Joey was my first cousin. On behalf of my beloved mother and my first cousin, I plead with the President and the Congress to accept the NIH report on the medical value of embryonic stem cell research and to not block federal funding for this promising, life-saving research.

Ramstad continued,

> it is too late for my dear mother and my deceased cousin, but it is not too late for 100 million other American people counting on the President and the Congress to give them hope. Let us give them hope. Let us give them life. Let us support funding for life-saving and life-extending embryonic stem cell research. It is clearly, clearly the right thing to do. (July 17, 2001, H4101)

Frist's comparison of embryonic nuclear transfer to abortion of a fetus was echoed by several members. Randall (Duke) Cunningham (R-CA) described how a personal experience affected him. "John Porter once . . . asked me to chair a committee [dealing] with children with exotic diseases. I had to shut down the committee it hurt so much. One little girl said, 'Congressman, you are the only person that can save my life,' and that little child died, and there are thousands of these children." Even that vivid experience was not convincing enough to override Cunningham's deeper fear about the slippery slope from stem cell experimentation to abortion. Like some others in his party, Cunningham wished to erect safeguards to limit research to discarded embryos.

> I am 100 percent pro-life, 11 years, but I support stem cell research of discarded cells. The concern that all of us have is [that] the same thing will happen that happened in England. They started with stem cell research, then they expanded it to nuclear transfer of the somatic cells. Then they went to human cloning, and even a subspecies so that they can use body parts. Where does it stop? The only way that we can control this research through the Federal Government is to make sure that these ethical and moral values are adhered to. We have to stop it here. (July 31, 2001, H4935)

If these personal appeals are more than grandstanding, they ought to be reflected in behavior as well as rhetoric. Table 5.7 analyzes the roll call vote on H.R. 2505, the Human Cloning Prohibition Act. The specification is almost identical to that used in earlier models. The results show first that ideological concerns were certainly salient. In contrast to the Charitable Choice analysis, district preferences are significant and positive, indicating that legislators from more conservative districts were also more likely to support the bill. Legislators' own ideological voting patterns were also strong predictors of the vote, as is expected. Indeed, to the degree that overall voting habits measured with NOMINATE also include the effects of religious values and other factors, this coefficient reveals the effects of both ideology directly and other factors indirectly. Removing NOMINATE from the model makes every other coefficient highly significant. While neither including nor excluding the measure is an ideal solution, retaining the variable provides for a much stricter test of my argument.

Among the personal characteristics measured, sex demonstrates a significant effect. All else constant, men were more likely to vote for the bill. Members from conservative districts and with conservative ideologies are also much more likely to cast a vote in favor of the cloning ban. Religious affiliations show mixed effects. Relative to other denominations, Jews and mainline Protestants were less likely to support the bill. The dummy variable for other/unaffiliated members is also significant and negative. In retrospect it seems sensible that these more liberal denominations were less supportive of the cloning ban than their Catholic and evangelical counterparts.

As is canonical in my approach, I now divide the results by party, reestimating the regression model separately for Democrats and Republicans as a proxy for those defending and challenging the status quo. Although the small sample sizes within each party weaken the statistical power of the models, table 5.8 shows some clear asymmetries. Gender and district ideology matter more for Democrats, but public ideology and

Table 5.7
Vote on Human Cloning Prohibition Act

Catholic	−1.06 (.72)
Jewish	−2.98** (1.00)
White Evangelical	−1.50 (.93)
White Mainline	−2.06** (.78)
Black Protestant	−.78 (.77)
Other Religion or Unaffiliated	−2.31* (1.17)
Female	−1.71** (.50)
South	.37 (.39)
District Ideology (Bush %)	.05** (.02)
Public Ideology (NOMINATE)	3.12** (.38)
Number of Cases	426
Log Likelihood	−131.44

Note: Logistic regression with standard errors in parentheses. Constant suppressed.
* $p < .05$, ** $p < .01$, one-tailed test.

religious affiliation once again were more predictive for Republicans. In contrast to Swers's (2002) results, I find that sex is more determinative for Democrats; women in that party were especially likely to oppose the bill. Democrats were also somewhat sensitive to the ideological concerns for their districts. In contrast, Republicans cast votes largely along ideological and religious lines. NOMINATE has a powerful influence on the vote, but so does religion, with more liberal denominations voting against the bill, although only among Republicans. Although Republicans brought the bill to the floor, their intent was to ward off scientific exploration that they deemed unethical. The legislation was an effort to stop the march toward full-fledged cloning and genetic modification of human beings. It is

TABLE 5.8
Vote on Human Cloning Prohibition Act, by Party

Explanatory Variable	*Democrats*	*Republicans*
Catholic	1.406	−10.297**
	(1.081)	(3.229)
Jewish	−1.217	−14.289
	(1.400)	(7.640)
White Evangelical	−.515	—
	(1.234)	
White Mainline	.415	−12.663**
	(1.081)	(3.602)
Black Protestant	2.497*	—
	(1.1.77)	
Other Religion or Unaffiliated	.809	−11.630**
	(1.620)	(3.387)
Female	−2.661*	.003
	(1.077)	(.952)
South	−.272	−1.404
	(.523)	(1.101)
District Ideology (Bush %)	.046*	.030
	(.019)	(.057)
Public Ideology (NOMINATE)	8.039**	21.273**
	(1.562)	(5.545)
Number of Cases	206	218
Log Likelihood	−72.694	−30.294

Note: Logistic regression with standard errors in parentheses. Empty cells indicate variables dropped due to insufficient cases or variation. Constant suppressed.

* $p < .05$, ** $p < .01$, one-tailed test.

little surprise that religious and ideological factors mattered more for Republicans, as they did in other cases in this chapter.

Conclusion

By the late 1990s, a spate of bioethical and religious issues appeared on the congressional agenda. It is probably not coincidental that Republicans won control of Congress in 1994. At least some of the rise in morality issues was due to exogenous technological change, such as claims by scientists that they had successfully cloned an animal, and so preceded Republican ascendance. The Republican Party leadership dealt with these matters as they arose but also addressed other issues such as partial birth abortion that would have otherwise gone unattended. While some of this new attention is due to the critical place of the Christian Right in the Republican Party, individual legislators' activities were also driven by their own religious views.

My view of religion is a narrow one that does not account for all of the ways that it might shape legislative behavior. A person's views about morality certainly extend beyond his stated religious denomination to include facets such as faith, devotion, importance of beliefs, and dogmatism. Moreover, values have many origins, among which religious orientation is but one. However important, these items are unfortunately beyond the scope of my measurement at the congressional level. My reliance in this chapter on a simple denominational family coding is crude and surely understates the role of religious values on legislative activity. The findings presented here and in other chapters should be considered the most minimal of evidence that personal factors shape legislative activity.

District preferences and the legislator's public ideology both have important effects on roll call votes dealing with matters of religion and bioethics. But aside from the highly partisan Charitable Choice vote, the effects are not entirely determinative of the bills I examined. Other factors enter into the member's voting calculus and should be considered as noteworthy aberrations from a one-dimensional view of congressional preferences. When pure ideological divisions recede in importance on particular votes, other forces become more influential.

More importantly, the impact of ideology tended to wane as I moved from floor votes to proactive indicators such as speechmaking and bill sponsorship. Sometimes district and legislator ideologies failed to explain those activities at all, leaving those who consult the recent scholarly literature on Congress without much guidance. But even when they remained statistically significant predictors, their effects were tempered by other influences, many of them tied to the personal backgrounds of members. Ideological and background variables often showed asymmetric effects, depending on which side of the issue a member was located. My analyses of issues of morality and religious freedom demonstrate in yet another policy domain that district preferences do not determine a legislator's action entirely, even on roll call votes. Shirking from constituent wishes happens, and the discretion enjoyed by legislators grows as one moves upstream in the legislative process, revealing that the personal roots of representation are greatest at earlier stages of policy formulation.

CHAPTER SIX

Conclusion

It is no surprise to even casual observers of Congress that U.S. Senators Rick Santorum and Arlen Specter have different policy preferences. What might be more surprising to students of Congress is that these differences do not stem primarily from partisanship and constituency but instead from who these senators are. Both are Republicans representing Pennsylvania, so neither of the usual suspects, party and constituency, is helpful in explaining why Santorum and Specter do what they do in Washington. One might go further by adding ideological preferences as a third factor, but this step merely black-boxes all of the other influences on legislative behavior. Investigating the two senators a bit more, we find that deeply held Catholic values guide Santorum's positions against abortion, gay marriage, and stem cell research. In Specter's case personal expertise and self-interest from his own cancer scares guide his activism on medical research and health care. Although their cases may be somewhat unusual, they illustrate just how powerful personal factors can be, not only in shaping their positions, which clearly differ, but their choices about which issues to tackle with the limited time and resources they have.

Through both qualitative and quantitative evidence I have demonstrated the personal roots of congressional representation. Anecdotes from the Hill, personal reflections in floor speeches, and my own interviews with former members strongly suggest that legislators' backgrounds influence their behavior. I highlighted a number of cases where the media believed members' personal views and life experiences guided their actions, sometimes in unexpected ways. In the heightened partisan environment of the modern Congress, the strange bedfellows created when members cross the aisle are often only possible because of personal motivation. In floor rhetoric and in substantial interviews with former members of Congress, I also detected great potential for personal traits to motivate legislative behavior. My theory of legislative preferences acknowledges personal factors and specifies the ways in which they shape legislative behavior along with other internal and external cues.

The quantitative evidence provides even stronger support for the theory. In studies of three different policy areas, I found that personal traits were important explanatory variables. Rather than simply concluding that personal factors "matter," I showed that they were often effective in precisely the ways my theory hypothesized. Tobacco use, educational choices, and religious views became better predictors of legislative action when the action was proactive rather than reactive, when specific bills rather than collections of bills were studied, and when legislators faced a threat to the status quo rather than acted as advocates for change. The tobacco chapter was the most comprehensive of the three, demonstrating the many asymmetries that pervade the lawmaking process and showing that even campaign donors respond to personal traits in unequal ways. The chapter on education policy found that personal choices about where representatives educate their children affected legislative action on educational bills, but that the effect was contingent on partisanship. The final application showed that religion motivated actions on ethical and religious freedom bills, more so for Republicans than Democrats. Although no single application can test all of the hypotheses that flow from the theory, together they provide compelling evidence that the theory is plausible and allows future congressional scholars to account for legislators' personal views in a more direct and consistent manner.

Limits to the Analysis

As with any project that steps outside of the existing paradigm, I will not have convinced all readers. Rather than view this book as the final word on the subject, my goal is to draw attention to neglected elements in congressional decision-making and lay out core propositions to guide later research. The theory offered here alerts scholars to the fact that members of Congress bring their experiences to office, where they affect behavior, just as all people rely on personal understandings in making choices. The typical person chooses which alternative to prefer but how active to be in pursing it. In a similar fashion, representatives' personal traits become more influential with respect to specific bills, when a legislator's position requires defense, and in the earlier stages of the lawmaking process. This is a new theory that deserves further refinement and elaboration beyond this book.

Empirical scrutiny of the theory should go further. I view the three case studies in this book as a demonstration of its plausibility, not as proof that it is absolutely correct in every setting. The tobacco application in chapter 3 is the most complete; the other applications lack data that could shed further light on the theory's predictions. Even when data on bill sponsorship and speechmaking are available, they represent only the most visible forms of lawmaking. The researcher cannot in a systematic way observe behind-the-scenes negotiation and lobbying, but the measurable behaviors that occur upstream in the process are reasonable proxies for them (Hall 1996). With notable exceptions, the general relationship is this: the greater the selectivity of participation, the stronger the effects of personal factors.

Finally, some may raise concern that the three policy applications studied here do not adequately represent the range of issues considered by Congress. Although they do not come close to exhausting the contemporary policy space, I am confident that tobacco, education, and religious and bioethical issues have been extremely salient in recent years. In George W. Bush's administration alone, one need look for evidence no further than the No Child Left Behind Act, congressional intervention in the tragic Terri Schiavo life support case, and Bush's veto of federal support for embryonic stem cell research. I concede that the domains I analyze probably contain more emotion and less history than routine legislation such as foreign policy and particularly the annual budget process. In the parlance of political science, my applications tilt toward "easy" issues more than "hard" issues (Carmines and Stimson 1989; Hurley and Hill 2003), toward moral more than technical (Mooney 1999), and toward novel more than established (Mansbridge 1999). Although my choices of applications were driven in part by timeliness and the data available, it is possible that these biases lead to the inadvertent overstatement of personal influences on legislative behavior. Yet I believe that the relationships identified in this book persist across a wide variety of applications. Additional research will help determine the conditions under which the theory holds.

Elections and Representation

If legislative behavior has a personal component, then it seems quite natural that voters might consider candidates' backgrounds when casting votes for members of Congress. Indeed, I would suggest that the personal characteristics of legislators can be valuable cues to voters. Consistent with Popkin's (1994) notion of gut-level rationality, I find that candidates' traits convey meaningful information to constituents about the actions they are likely to take in office. Research shows that voters do in fact use descriptive information about candidates to make choices, making inferences based on visible traits (Koch 2000; McDermott 2005; Sanbonmatsu 2002b). It is perhaps unsurprising that descriptive characteristics often provide reasonable clues in determining the representative's political orientation.

Like Popkin, I move beyond the traditional categories of interest—race and sex—to examine a wider range of experiences, interests, and expertise. Traits such as race and gender are easily gleaned from campaign materials and even a candidate's name as it is listed on the ballot. Less visible traits such as religion, sexual orientation, and wealth typically require more effort on the voter's part to discern. Candidates may emphasize issues on which they have some personal background, and voters may well respond to these connections (Sellers 1998). As I have shown, these factors often interact with the traditional categories of race, gender, and party affiliation in swaying voters' decisions.

Much of the scholarly literature assumes that a candidate's race or gender is used as a shortcut to compensate for limited information. That is, a voter's knowing that a candidate is African-American substitutes for direct knowledge about her policy positions and priorities. Viewed in this way, a candidate's traits are helpful information to a voter, but less meaningful than knowledge of indicators such as her ideology or partisanship. This analysis of voters' thinking would more often be accurate if voters cared only about the general ideology of the candidate. However, many voters, as members of issue publics, are concerned with specific policy areas. Because specific traits relate to specific policies, in such cases knowing the characteristics of the candidate might be viewed as a way to overcome the limited information provided by partisanship, ideology, and other general indicators.

I noted in chapter 2 the ways in which descriptive representation is beneficial in ways beyond affecting legislators' responsiveness to their constituents' preferences. Research has shown that descriptive representation increases trust in government and participation by adequately represented groups. To the degree that voter participation is rewarded with more government largesse (Martin 2003), these psychological benefits might also translate into policy payoffs. Even if this full chain of events connecting citizen involvement with policy responsiveness does not take place, merely increasing citizens' connections with their representatives is a desirable by-product of descriptive representation (Mansbridge 1999). At the collective level descriptive representation seems only fair as a standard, especially if other qualities need not be sacrificed to achieve it. At the dyadic level I have studied, collective descriptive representation seems an important ingredient for maintaining acceptable levels of engagement across many subconstituencies, but it does not guarantee responsiveness of any one legislator to his constituency. Without perfectly homogeneous constituencies—which are neither desirable nor possible—representatives will never emulate their constituents exactly. Altering the conduct of elections via redistricting reform would be one way to adjust the discrepancies between legislators and constituents, but no amount of tinkering can eliminate what is an inherent discord in any representative republic.

My interest in descriptive representation goes beyond these procedural benefits to understand how substantive democracy is shaped by legislators' personal traits. Descriptive representation is not necessarily antagonistic toward or even independent from substantive representation. The two are especially entwined in policy realms where a legislator's background is highly relevant.

The power of descriptive representation is greatest in the earliest stages of the policy process. Whereas the literature on shirking implies that a representative comes up short when he fails to represent the voters' wishes, my approach highlights legislators whose actions are independent of what their constituents want. Rather than shy away to avoid controversy, legislators devote precious time to policies that connect to their own values. Scholars need to be aware of this regularity, of course, but so do voters who wish to see their policy interests represented in Washington.

To influence public policy, voters would be well advised to choose candidates who are "like them" on as wide a variety of dimensions as possible. In selecting the right "type" of representative, ideology and partisanship are obviously important considerations, but so are demographic characteristics. Selection of a faithful agent at the outset is superior to monitoring an unfaithful one between elections. Few legislators are genuinely motivated to act of out electoral fear, and elections are imperfect mechanisms for sending signals to Congress. On particular issues, where individual legislators typically matter most, representatives cannot be easily monitored and disciplined by their principals, that is, their constituents. A more effective and efficient approach is for the agent to choose a like-minded principal in the first place. The more intensely a voter cares about an issue, the more he should seek a representative who shares his interest in it.

Might more competitive elections enhance representation? The answer to this question is a qualified yes. It is qualified for two reasons. First, the question presupposes that more policy representation is always a good thing. However, what is to one observer responsiveness is to another merely pandering, and is not a particularly noble goal (Jacobs and Shapiro 2000). Greater responsiveness to constituents also implies smaller differences between candidates' platforms and less room for deliberation and expertise to enter as legislators consider policies. Few would wish to encourage these sins just to increase the median voter's utility.

Second, there is no guarantee that competition will enhances representation. Even perfectly competitive elections would not remove all slack in the constituent-representative relationship. Because of the diversity of viewpoints and priorities among voters, not all constituents can be adequately represented by a single representative. Even two candidates cannot account for the range of opinions and backgrounds in the electorate. As I explained in chapter 2, elections are an important yet imperfect mechanism for voters to convey their policy demands to the legislature. Elections are often about just a few issues, not the full range of matters that a representative will encounter. A trait that seems irrelevant at the time of an election may come to be crucial in an upcoming debate over policy. House campaigns tend to focus on the candidates' character and attentiveness to the district rather than issues. These factors are not easily dismissed as inconsequential. Representatives' efforts to identify with constituents by appearing to be "one of them" is a common way to highlight shared backgrounds (Fenno 1978). It conveys precisely the values, information, and self-interests that motivate the personal roots of representation. Voters who choose a candidate out of a sense of shared identity may be acting just as rationally as those voting on the basis of ideological proximity alone. Choosing a candidate with whom one identifies may be a shrewd policy decision, whether or not it is intended as such.

Whether they feature policy stances or not, congressional campaigns often fail to meet the standards of full competition in other ways. Most elections pit a strong incumbent against a weak challenger and thus fail to offer a genuine choice. Moreover, there is mixed evidence about the degree to which stiff competition induces Downsian-style moderation by candidates. As discussed in chapter 2, hearty competition draws candidates a bit closer to the ideological center, but substantial divergence usually remains (Ansolabehere, Snyder, and Stewart 2001a; Burden 2004a; Fiorina 1974). Moreover, a debate rages about whether competitive districts actually produce more moderate candidates (Ansolabehere, Snyder, and Stewart 2001a; Bishin 2005; Burden 2004a; Fiorina 1974; Gulati 2004; Huntington 1950; King 2003). Thus, it is not clear that harder-fought elections would always yield more substantive representation, if that is the most desirable end state.

The Desirability of Shirking

The discussion to this point raises the question of just how much discretion should be granted to elected officials. The political economy literature on shirking is unequivocal in its assumption that deviating from voters' opinions is undesirable. When a representative acts independently, scholars imply that constituents are being short-changed by lobbying groups or the legislator's self-interest. From this point of view, any divergence between constituents and representatives is intolerable. As I have argued, however, legislators deviate from their districts' interests in response to a host of internal and external forces. Only sound theoretical reasoning and empirical testing can determine whether seemingly insidious forces such as self-interest are responsible for shirking, or other, more redeeming sources of preferences, such as information, values, or even partisanship, underlie it. To recall an earlier analogy, it is critical to distinguish the good cholesterol from the bad. Divergence from the opinions of constituents is itself inherently neither good or bad. Only by decomposing the quite regular deviations from public opinion can the analyst judge whether they occur for the right or the wrong reasons.

In this vein, it is important to recall my point that deviation from district opinion is more in evidence on individual bills than it is when aggregating votes across many bills. For the researcher who studies only voting scales or general patterns, shirking will appear less frequent and district preferences more important than I have suggested. In this way highly aggregated studies, which attempt to generalize, actually produce selective results. For the interest groups, voters, politicians, and academics who care about policy outcomes, actions on *individual* bills are critical. The usual predictors of legislative behavior, such as ideology, partisanship, and district preferences, lose much of their predictive power when one considers individual bills, and when one moves upstream in the legislative process, where participation is more selective. Shirking in these settings can be reduced by electoral competitiveness, the homogeneity of district preferences, and other factors, but it happens nonetheless. Rather than measure the degree of shirking, I instead stipulate that shirking is an inherent part of representative government. More fruitful inquiries ask *why* shirking happens, to render judgments about how it affects the health of the democratic system (Mansbridge 2003). Although the term *shirking* carries negative connotations, I believe that deviating from public opinion is not always undesirable. For that reason, we might just as well leave shirking behind and instead identify the factors that contribute to correspondence with or deviation from constituent preferences.

Deviation from the median voter's position may then be evaluated as desirable or undesirable depending on its *causes*. Looking back at the four factors I proposed as sources of legislative preferences—values, expertise, self-interest, and ideology—one may render normative judgments about each. Two of the four factors seem entirely reasonable, perhaps even noble, reasons for policy deviation. One would be viewed as undesirable by nearly every observer, and the status of the final one depends on one's view of representative democracy, particularly what voters ought to be choosing when they pick a candidate.

From my point of view, a legislator who draws upon his own values and personal information is doing a service to his constituents. Personal information, however limited, can be quite valuable to a lawmaker just as it is to everyday decision-making by everyone else. When the information comes from an exhaustive review of evidence, it becomes expertise and thus allows the representative to ask as a trustee. When the information is based on firsthand experience, the data are often more selective but also more meaningful. Having been a schoolteacher, athlete, minister, lawyer, or parent provides a legislator with insights about the profession, albeit from a perspective that has the potential to be overly narrow. Yet this direct experience keeps the legislator in touch with society and allows her to evaluate policy proposals in light of these memorable interactions. Biases surely creep in when a former schoolteacher, for example, fails to see the classroom setting from the perspective of the principal or superintendent, but the firsthand experiences of dealing with curricula, handling student problems, and being embedded in a policy-relevant environment are still useful and may overcome biases of narrow perspective. The general experiences that legislators have as consumers, parents, children, homeowners, motorists, litigants, and employees are invaluable.

In contrast to information, using values to construct legislative preferences occupies slightly more ambiguous normative territory. A rigid, dogmatic approach to public policy such as Congressman Ron Paul's (R-TX) libertarian worldview can be constraining if it rules out reasonable alternatives. A thoughtful and compelling personal value such as Representative Tony Hall's (D-OH) concern about hunger might also rule out pragmatic compromises, but its origin in his experiences makes it feel more acceptable. Although defenders of abortion rights balk at Senator Rick Santorum's (R-PA) views on the issue, the fact that his activism derives from deeply personal experience of a premature dead child and his Catholic faith allows even opponents to understand the intensity of his views. Not all values are acceptable to all constituents, and some values can lead to rather different policy prescriptions, depending on their interpretation. A legislator's personal values nonetheless provide a fair foundation upon which to establish positions and criteria for taking legislative action. Voters can be made aware of them during election campaigns and choose candidates whose values they support. Like ideologies, values are generally broad and hierarchical in that they determine views on specific policies, yet they are often less rigid than prepackaged ideologies. A Congress that made decisions based on values would surely be more palatable than one driven solely by partisanship or career concerns.

The third personal motive, self-interest, is the least acceptable source of legislative preferences. A legislator who pursues a tax cut mainly because it would increase his income is not especially enlightened, concerned about the public good, or relying on a wide base of information about the policy's consequences. A smoker who opposes tobacco regulation not because of principles but out of selfish concerns is equally primitive. Self-interest might work a general motivation for legislative preferences only if members of the legislature fairly represented the population. Much as with older notions of pluralism, even self-oriented policymakers could produce policies that meet with constituents' approval. But self-interest may be a weapon when the Congress does not look like the people it represents. Because members of Congress tend to be older, wealthier, whiter, better educated, and are more often married, policies based on their self-interest come at the expense of constituents who fall at the other end of the demographic scale. Just in terms of the of the three policy applications analyzed here, we discovered that representatives were less likely than the public to smoke, more likely to have children in private school, and more likely to be mainline Protestants and Jewish. If legislative action, especially proactive behavior, were based only on self-interest derived from these descriptive categories, the substantial shirking I observed would be unpalatable. If, as I reasoned was more likely, smoking habits and school choices and religious affiliations indicate something broader about a legislator's values and expertise, they become more tolerable sources of policy deviation.

The final source of legislative preferences—ideology—plays a supporting role in my analysis. This is primarily because the question of ideology has been studied so extensively that it needs little additional exploration. The distinction I make is in pointing out that ideology is but one component of raw legislative preferences. The higher the levels of abstraction and aggregation, the more important ideology appears. I argue that some of this relationship is merely tautology or inertia; a collection of votes predicts another collection of votes quite well (Burden, Caldeira, and Groseclose 2000; Jackson and Kingdon 1992). Moreover, legislators report their positions as being somewhat different than their roll call records suggests (Ansolabehere, Snyder, and Stewart 2001a; Burden 2004a), so it is hard to know precisely what roll call patterns measure besides roll call patterns.

Ideology (or partisanship, depending on one's interpretation of aggregate voting scores) becomes more highly correlated with behavior the more passive the member's participation. Because roll call votes come at the end of the legislative process, their complexity and dimensionality has been reduced by party leaders and others who control the agenda, which in turn often elevates the salience of partisan considerations over other factors that influenced earlier stages of the process. Because they explain so much of roll call outcomes, to show that personal traits affect votes once ideology and district preferences have been controlled is a real challenge. Nonetheless, this is precisely what my three policy applications do.

Whether one values partisan ideology as a component of legislative preferences is a matter of taste. Many political scientists support the "responsible party" or Westminster model in which party labels constrain a politician's actions, as exemplified in the 1950 American Political Science Association report. In its most extreme form, a legislator is nothing but a party pawn who must support its position in every situation. One might soften this view by acknowledging that parties' positions are based on input from its members, so the process of policy formulation and legislator support is in fact partially endogenous (Cox and McCubbins 1993; Downs 1957). But this is not the American system and never will be, given the autonomy of candidates, use of primaries to choose party nominees, and separately elected presidency (Mayhew 1974; Wattenberg 1991). Recent ideological polarization in Congress, which has heightened party voting, has been widely criticized as unnatural and inefficient (Dionne 1991). Ironically, it is a manifestation of the responsible party model that the discipline earlier endorsed (Fiorina 1999). Of course, clarity and faithfulness in party platforms need not lead to polarization. The APSA report emphasized differentiation between candidates' positions, but not so much as to label them extreme. Consistent differences between candidates are to be lauded but large chasms between the parties are harmful.

If academics want to have it both ways, surely the public is of two minds about ideology as well. Voters wish to have candidates who are responsive to their preferences but are also above pandering on the basis of the latest public opinion poll (Hibbing and Theiss-Morse 2002). The advantage of ideology as a consideration is that it can usually be determined before an election. Most candidates for Congress have voting records in the state legislature, have been active in earlier policy debates, and convey their positions via campaign communications. Although elections remain an imperfect mechanism for inducing compliance with constituents' desires, they can be vehicles for choosing legislators who already share the general views of the voters. Especially if voters care about the aggregate voting records of their representatives, ideology is a wise cue to use in selection. In line with my argument about the critical importance of candidate selection, it has been changing patterns of candidate recruitment that are responsible for most of the polarization of Congress over the last couple of decades (King 1997; Poole and Rosenthal 1997; Rohde 1991; Stonecash, Brewer, and Mariani 2002).

I have argued that the relative importance of these four factors changes as one moves upstream in the policy process and as one disaggregates a series of actions into isolated policy choices. In relocating the focus of the analysis in these two ways, the personal factors of values, information, and self-interest grow in importance. At the same time, a legislator's behavior becomes more consequential. One vote out of 435 is not likely to matter much on a bill. Moving up or down a tick or two on an interest group's rating of votes is unlikely to have any real policy consequences. Yet one proactive legislator on a piece of legislation can affect its fate quite dramatically. It is at these points when personal concerns become more salient, making descriptive representation more important and the substantive wishes of constituents and other influences less potent. Policy representation faces stiffer tests exactly when the representative becomes more important to the legislative outcome.

Revisiting Representatives' Personal Traits

I have argued that who legislators are when they arrive in office can explain much of their legislative behavior. Without the benefit of my theory, the spotty findings that emerged from earlier research on blacks and women in Congress are puzzling. Previous studies found that the effects of race and sex were unpredictable. No theory was available to make sense of these results within a single unified framework. The review of this literature in chapter 2 suggests that the patterns of results fit quite nicely with my predictions. To the extent that one can generalize from a modest number of studies, race and sex are better predictors of proactive behavior than of reactive behavior, and are often contingent on party affiliation or other legislative cleavages, displaying the same asymmetries that I discovered in other applications. I would expect similar relationships using different characteristics of legislators.

Because descriptive representation is most relevant precisely at the points in the legislative process when action is most consequential, the degree to which the House of Representatives mirrors characteristics in the electorate is a real concern. There are two structural factors affecting the degree of congruence between legislators and their constituents: the overall percentage of the electorate possessing a trait and the degree of geographic segregation around the demographic trait.

Consider again the two most common cases in the literature, sex and race. Sex is distributed almost equally across congressional districts. Men and women live among one another and each set is approximately 50% of the electorate. Half of the population will thus be represented by a member of the other sex, regardless of the composition of Congress. What will vary is the degree to which this mismatch involves male or female constituents. The current Congress is 14% female and consequently underrepresents women significantly. A legislature with an equal split of men and women would have the same overall rate of congruence but with both male and female constituents having the same chance of being represented by a legislator of their sex.

In contrast, African-Americans, who are geographically concentrated in the South and urban areas in other parts of the country, are a clear minority at roughly 13% of the population. It would be possible for the legislature to mirror the population collectively in the sense that the percentage of black legislators was the same as the percentage of black Americans. The current Congress is actually close to this milestone. Yet aggregate parity could still translate into significant discord when the legislator-constituent dyad is considered. In addition, the severe geographic segregation of blacks and whites ironically enhances the possibility of matching constituent and legislator traits. This is why racially motivated redistricting has been so controversial. Districting so as to pack minorities into urban districts and whiten surrounding districts can have precisely this effect. As my review in chapter 2 suggests, it remains a matter of opinion whether maximizing substantive representation is desirable if it reduces the overall number of minority lawmakers.

More often than not, a descriptive trait is distributed more like race than sex: geographically segregated and imbalanced between those who display it and those who do not. In applications in this book, I found that smokers were underrepresented at the aggregate level, but that the smoking habits of legislators and their constituents were usually the same. In terms of religion, descriptive representation was far less common. At the aggregate level, white evangelicals were vastly underrepresented, but mainline Protestants and small denominations were overrepresented. At the district level, roughly two-thirds of constituents were represented by a legislator from a different denominational family, a high level of discord for a trait that displays a sizable dose of geographic definition. The point is that the distribution of traits in the electorate put logical bounds on the degree to which constituents can be represented by legislators who look like them.

Candidate selection is important because the window created by the election campaign is perhaps the best opportunity for the voter to influence government. Only rarely can lobbying by constituents, interest groups, or other actors change a legislator's behavior in a consequential way. Although interest groups are created in part to influence the lawmaking process, they often monitor and reward sympathetic legislators as much as they persuade reluctant ones. The public lacks the time, knowledge, interest, and other resources necessary to follow even the most visible actions by their representatives (Delli Carpini and Keeter 1996; Hibbing and Theiss-Morse 2002).

Substantive representation becomes more possible during governing periods if subconstituencies or issue publics are responsible for monitoring individual issues (Arnold 1990; Bishin 2000; Converse 1964; Hutchings 2003). The stepping down from full constituency monitoring of all legislative actions to selective monitoring by particularly affected subconstituencies might induce greater accountability, but this is merely a move toward interest group pluralism in which the groups do not represent the full universe of interests. It is no longer the median voter in the district who controls the legislator but the opinions of a hodgepodge of interests, which are almost certainly not representative of the average voter. The constituents who care most about corn subsidies, foreign policy toward the Middle East, corporate tax rates, and malpractice insurance are sure to be "high demanders" with preferences that lie some distance away from the political center. Thus, even a division of labor among influential subconstituencies does not force a legislator to heed district opinion. Selection of a like-minded representative on election day remains the most potent means for inducing responsiveness.

Campaign Money and Representation

Much popular alarm has been raised about the role of money in politics. It is often believed that donors who do not represent the average voter are able to influence legislators unfairly by lining their pockets or funding their opponents (Grant and Rudolph 2004; Hibbing and Theiss-Morse 2002). I challenged this view, finding little evidence in the academic literature that money can buy roll call votes (Ansolabehere, de Figueiredo, and Snyder 2003; Hall and Wayman 1990; Roscoe and Jenkins 2005). Like voters, interest groups and other donors maximize their influence by affecting candidate selection (typically in the form of incumbent retention) rather than by spending large sums to alter the behavior of those already in office.

Although I dismiss the widespread impact of money on legislative behavior, I identified critical ways in which campaign funds are tied to representation. My analyses of tobacco and education in chapters 3 and 4 showed that PACs were aware of representatives' personal traits when they were relevant to the interest group's preferred policies. Tobacco PACs gave more money to smoking members, less to nonsmokers. Teachers' unions gave more money to legislators with children in public schools, less to those with children in private schools. I cannot determine whether interest groups glean this information directly or the relationships appear "as if" groups steered donations on the basis of candidates' personal traits, yet the former explanation is viable given the large number of controls used in the regression models.

Regardless of the precise mechanism, legislators' personal traits do influence the funds they receive. Although the money might not influence legislative behavior, it does affect whether they remain in office to continue their legislative efforts. Incumbents raise large sums of money to scare away strong opponents. This in turn makes elections less competitive and encourages legislators' personal links to policy. Voters should thus care about candidates' personal traits for a second reason. Not only do they affect their legislative activities, they also affect their chances at reelection, which in turn affects the degree to which elections are effective means of policy control, a double whammy.

Personal Roots of Representation

This book asks legislative scholars to reexamine what is meant by legislative preferences. A careful analysis of preferences can reveal the relative weight of ideology, partisanship, voters' interests relative to the representative's values, self-interest, and expertise that for the last decade or two have been relegated to a black box by the scholarly community.

Reverting to the common assumption that preferences are nothing more than the internalization of constituents' ideological demands is reasonable when a scholar examines roll call votes taken on many issues. It becomes less tenable as the mix of influences changes across individual bills and when one focuses further upstream in the legislative process.

The convincingness of this argument depends on whether representatives actually care about making good policy and have personal motivations for doing so. I tried to demonstrate this necessity through qualitative analysis of floor rhetoric and quantitative analysis of votes, speeches, and bill cosponsorship. As a final piece of evidence, I ask the reader to consider the occupational choices of legislators once they have left office. Fenno (1978) has already pointed out that a relatively small number of representatives have "Potomac Fever," most returning to their home states after leaving the House. I would add that many former members of Congress, even those who remain in Washington, pursue careers that are connected in some way to their personal backgrounds.

As institutionally thick and partisan as the current Congress might be, its occupants continue to be human beings who bring their values, expertise, self-interests, and ideologies with them to office. Legislative preferences contain all of these elements. Although party leaders, the president, and other actors lobby representatives, in the end representatives must decide what their positions will be and how active they should be in advocating them. Their personal preferences are key in these making these public choices. As Senator Warren Rudman put it (see the epigraph to chapter 2), members of Congress represent the "sum total of life's experiences," and these experiences have the power to shape legislative activities. Personal experiences help legislators make sense of debates over policy by providing frames for proposals. They increase confidence in legislative decisions by linking vivid events from members' personal histories to the consequences that flow from a bill. These experiences are often captured by descriptive traits, which become more important as legislating becomes more active, selective, defensive, and specific. Though scholars have portrayed the process of representation as mechanical and structural, it is also personal.

References

Achen, Christopher H. 1978. "Measuring Representation." *American Journal of Political Science* 22:475–510.

Alvarez, R. Michael, and John Brehm. 2002. *Hard Choices, Easy Answers: Values, Information, and American Public Opinion.* Princeton, NJ: Princeton University Press.

Amer, Mildred L. 1999. "Membership of the 106th Congress: A Profile." Congressional Research Service Report RS20013.

Ansolabehere, Stephen, John M. de Figueiredo, and James M. Snyder Jr. 2003. "Why is There so Little Money in U.S. Politics?" *Journal of Economic Perspectives* 17:105–30.

Ansolabehere, Stephen, James M. Snyder Jr., and Charles Stewart III. 2001a. "Candidate Positioning in U.S. House Elections." *American Journal of Political Science* 45:136–59.

———. 2001b. "The Effects of Party and Preferences on Congressional Roll-Call Voting." *Legislative Studies Quarterly* 26:533–72.

Arnold, R. Douglas. 1990. *The Logic of Congressional Action.* New Haven: Yale University Press.

Arrow, Kenneth J. 1951. *Social Choice and Individual Values.* New Haven: Yale University Press.

Asher, Herbert B., and Herbert F. Weisberg. 1978. "Voting Change in Congress." *American Journal of Political Science* 22:391–425.

Banducci, Susan A., Todd Donovan, and Jeffrey A. Karp. 2004. "Minority Representation, Empowerment, and Participation." *Journal of Politics* 66:534–56.

Bauer, Raymond A., Ithiel de Sola Pool, and Lewis Anthony Dexter. 1963. *American Business and Public Policy.* New York: Atherton.

Baumgartner, Frank R., and Bryan D. Jones. 1993. *Agendas and Instability in American Politics.* Chicago: University of Chicago Press.

Bender, Bruce, and John R. Lott Jr. 1996. "Legislator Voting and Shirking: A Critical Review of the Literature." *Public Choice* 87:67–100.

Bernstein, Robert A. 1989. *Elections, Representatives, and Congressional Voting Behavior: The Myth of Constituency Control.* Englewood Cliffs, NJ: Prentice Hall.

Bianco, William T. 1992. "Representatives and Constituents in the Postreform Congress: The Problem of Persuasion." In *The Postreform Congress,* ed. Roger H. Davidson. New York: St. Martin's Press.

———. 1994. *Trust: Representatives and Constituents.* Ann Arbor: University of Michigan Press.

———. 2005. "Last Post for 'The Greatest Generation': The Policy Implications of the Decline of Military Experience in the U.S. Congress." *Legislative Studies Quarterly* 30:85–102.

Binder, Sarah A., Eric D. Lawrence, and Forrest Maltzman. 1999. "Uncovering the Hidden Effect of Party." *Journal of Politics* 61:815–31.

Bishin, Benjamin G. 2000. "Constituency Influence in Congress: Do Subconstituencies Matter?" *Legislative Studies Quarterly* 25:389–415.

———. 2005. "Competition and Congressional Representation: Are the Benefits of Elections Overstated?" Unpublished manuscript, University of Miami.

Box-Steffensmeier, Janet M. 1996. "A Dynamic Analysis of the Role of War Chests in Campaign Strategy." *American Journal of Political Science* 40:352–71.

Brady, David W., and Naomi Lynn. 1973. "Switched-Seat Congressional Districts: Their Effect on Party Voting and Public Policy." *American Journal of Political Science* 17:528–43.

Brady, David W., and Barbara Sinclair. 1984. "Building Majorities for Policy Change in the U.S. House: Conversion Versus Replacement." *Journal of Politics* 46:1033–1100.

Bratton, Kathleen A., and Kerry L. Haynie. 1999. "Agenda Setting and Legislative Success in State Legislatures: The Effects of Gender and Race." *Journal of Politics* 61:658–79.

Burden, Barry C. 2000. "Representation versus Self-Interest in U.S. Politics: The Cases of Tobacco Regulation and School Choice." Paper presented at the Annual Meeting of the American Political Science Association, Washington, DC.

———. 2004a. "Candidate Positioning in U.S. Congressional Elections." *British Journal of Political Science* 34:211–27.

———. 2004b. "A Technique for Estimating Candidate and Voter Locations." *Electoral Studies* 23:621–37.

Burden, Barry C., Gregory A. Caldeira, and Tim Groseclose. 2000. "Measuring the Ideologies of U.S. Senators: The Song Remains the Same." *Legislative Studies Quarterly* 25:237–58.

Burden, Barry C., and Aage R. Clausen. 1998. "The Unfolding Drama: Party and Ideology in the 104th House." In *Great Theatre: The American Congress in the 1990s,* ed. Herbert F. Weisberg and Samuel C. Patterson. New York: Cambridge University Press.

Burden, Barry C., and Tammy M. Frisby. 2004. "Preferences, Partisanship, and Whip Activity in the House of Representatives." *Legislative Studies Quarterly* 26:569–90.

Burns, Nancy, Kay Lehman Schlozman, and Sidney Verba. 2001. *The Private Roots of Public Action: Gender, Equality, and Political Participation.* Cambridge: Harvard University Press.

Cameron, Charles, David Epstein, and Sharyn O'Halloran. 1996. "Do Majority-Minority Districts Maximize Substantive Black Representation in Congress?" *American Political Science Review* 90:794–812.

Campbell, Andrea Louise. 2002. "Self-Interest, Social Security, and the Distinctive Participation Patterns of Senior Citizens." *American Political Science Review* 96:565–74.

Campbell, David E. 2006. "Religious 'Threat' in Contemporary Presidential Elections." *Journal of Politics* 68:104–15.

Canes-Wrone, Brandice, David W. Brady, and John F. Cogan. 2002. "Out of Step, Out of Office: Electoral Accountability and House Members' Voting." *American Political Science Review* 96:127–40.

Canon, David T. 1990. *Actors, Athletes, and Astronauts: Political Amateurs in the United States Congress.* Chicago: University of Chicago Press.

———. 1999. *Race, Redistricting, and Representation: The Unintended Consequences of Black Majority Districts.* Chicago: University of Chicago Press.

Carmines, Edward G., and James A. Stimson. 1989. *Issue Evolution: Race and the Transformation of American Politics.* Princeton, NJ: Princeton University Press.

Carson, Richard T., and Joe A. Oppenheimer. 1984. "A Method of Estimating the Personal Ideology of Political Representatives." *American Political Science Review* 78:163–78.

Chappell, Henry W., Jr. 1982. "Campaign Contributions and Congressional Voting: A Simultaneous Probit-Tobit Model." *Review of Economics and Statistics* 62:77–83.

Citrin, Jack, and Donald Philip Green. 1990. "The Self-Interest Motive in American Public Opinion." In *Research in Micropolitics,* vol. 3, ed. Samuel Long. Greenwich, CT: JAI Press.

Clinton, Joshua D. 2006. "Representation in Congress: Constituents and Roll Calls in the 106th House." *Journal of Politics* 68:397–409.

Clinton, Joshua D., Simon Jackman, and Douglas Rivers. 2004. "'The Statistical Analysis of Roll Call Data.'" *American Political Science Review* 98:355–70.

Cnudde, Charles F., and Donald J. McCrone. 1966. "The Linkage between Constituency Attitudes and Congressional Voting Behavior: A Causal Model." *American Political Science Review* 60:66–72.

Converse, Philip E. 1964. "The Nature of Belief Systems in Mass Publics." In *Ideology and Discontent,* ed. David E. Apter. New York: Free Press.

Cooper, Matthew. 1996. "Liberals for a Day." *New Republic.* May 20.

Cox, Gary W., and Mathew D. McCubbins. 1993. *Legislative Leviathan: Party Government in the House.* Berkeley and Los Angeles: University of California Press.

———. 2005. *Setting the Agenda: Responsible Party Government in the U.S. House of Representatives.* New York: Cambridge University Press.

Crile, George. 2003. *Charles Wilson's War: The Extraordinary Story of the Largest Covert Operation in History.* New York: Atlantic Monthly Press.

Davidson, Clifford. 2002. "Political Cytosis: The Fetal Stem Cell Debate in the Federal Legislature and What It Illustrates about Moral Debates over Technology." Undergraduate honors thesis, Harvard University.

de Guia, N. A., J. E. Cohen, M. J. Ashley, R. Ferrence, J. Rehm, D. T. Studlar, and D. Northrup. 2003. "Dimensions Underlying Legislator Support for Tobacco Control Policies." *Tobacco Control* 12:133–39.

Delli Carpini, Michael X., and Scott Keeter. 1996. *What Americans Know about Politics and Why It Matters.* New Haven: Yale University Press.

Derthick, Martha A. 2001. *Up in Smoke: From Legislation to Litigation in Tobacco Politics.* Washington, DC: CQ Press.

Dionne, E. J., Jr. 1991. *Why Americans Hate Politics.* New York: Simon and Schuster.

Downs, Anthony. 1957. *An Economic Theory of Democracy.* New York: Harper Collins.

Edwards, Mickey. 2003. "Political Science and Political Practice: The Pursuit of Grounded Inquiry." *Perspectives on Politics* 1:349–54.

Elster, Jon, and John E. Roemer, eds. 1993. *Interpersonal Comparisons of Well-Being.* New York: Cambridge University Press.

Erikson, Robert S. 1978. "Constituency Opinion and Congressional Behavior: A Reexamination of the Miller-Stokes Representation Data." *American Journal of Political Science* 22:511–35.

Erikson, Robert S., Michael B. MacKuen, and James A. Stimson. 2002. *The Macro Polity.* New York: Cambridge University Press.

Erikson, Robert S., and Gerald C. Wright. 2000. "Representation of Constituency Ideology in Congress." In *Continuity and Change in House Elections,* ed. David W. Brady, John F. Cogan, and Morris P. Fiorina. Palo Alto, CA: Stanford University Press.

Erikson, Robert S., Gerald C. Wright, and John P. McIver. 1993. *Statehouse Democracy: Public Opinion and Policy in the American States.* New York: Cambridge University Press.

Eulau, Heinz, and Paul D. Karps. 1977. "The Puzzle of Representation: Specifying Components of Responsiveness." *Legislative Studies Quarterly* 2:233–54.

Evans, C. Lawrence. 2002. "How Senators Decide: An Exploration." In *U.S. Senate Exceptionalism,* ed. Bruce I. Oppenheimer. Columbus: Ohio State University Press.

Evans, Jocelyn Jones. 2005. *Women, Partisanship, and the Congress.* New York: Palgrave Macmillan.

Fearon, James D. 1999. "Electoral Accountability and the Control of Politicians: Selecting Good Types versus Sanctioning Poor Performance." In *Democracy, Accountability, and Representation,* ed. Adam Przeworski, Susan C. Stokes, and Bernard Manin. New York: Cambridge University Press.

Feldman, Stanley. 1982. "Economic Self-Interest and Political Behavior." *American Journal of Political Science* 26:446–66.

———. 1988. "Structure and Consistency in Public Opinion: The Role of Core Beliefs and Values." *American Journal of Political Science* 32:416–40.

Fenno, Richard F., Jr. 1978. *Home Style: House Members in their Districts.* Boston: Little, Brown.

———. 1986. "Observation, Context, and Sequence in the Study of Politics." *American Political Science Review* 80:3–15.

———. 1991. *Learning to Legislate: The Senate Education of Arlen Specter.* Washington, DC: CQ Press.

Finn, Chester E., Jr., Bruno V. Manno, and Gregg Vanourek. 2001. *Charter Schools in Action: Renewing Public Education.* Princeton, NJ: Princeton University Press.

Fiorina, Morris P. 1974. *Representatives, Roll Calls, and Constituencies.* Lexington, MA: D. C. Heath.

———. 1989. *Congress: Keystone of the Washington Establishment.* 2nd ed. New Haven: Yale University Press.

———. 1999. "Whatever Happened to the Median Voter?" Paper presented at the MIT Conference on Parties and Congress.

Fordham, Benjamin O., and Timothy J. McKeown. 2003. "Selection and Influence: Interest Groups and Congressional Voting on Trade Policy." *International Organization* 57:519–49.

Fowler, Linda L. 1982. "How Interest Groups Select Issues for Rating Voting Records of Members of the U.S. Congress." *Legislative Studies Quarterly* 7:401–14.

Gay, Claudine. 2001. "The Effect of Black Congressional Representation on Political Participation." *American Political Science Review* 95:589–602.

———. 2002. "Spirals of Trust? The Effect of Descriptive Representation on the Relationship between Citizens and Their Government." *American Journal of Political Science* 46:717–33.

Goldstein, Adam O., Joanna E Cohen, Brian S. Flynn, Nel H. Gottlieb, Laura J. Solomon, Greg S. Dana, Karl E. Bauman, and Michael C. Munger. 1997. "State Legislators' Attitudes and Voting Intentions toward Tobacco Control Legislation." *American Journal of Public Health* 87:1197–1200.

Gooch, Lesli McCollum. 2004. "When Politics is Personal: The Role of Personal Policy Interests in Congressional Activity." Paper presented at the Annual Meeting of the Midwest Political Science Association, Chicago.

Goren, Paul. 2004. "Political Sophistication and Policy Reasoning: A Reconsideration." *American Journal of Political Science* 48:462–78.

Grant, J. Tobin, and Thomas J. Rudolph. 2004. *Expression vs. Equality: The Politics of Campaign Finance Reform.* Columbus: Ohio State University Press.

Green, Donald Philip, and Elizabeth Gerken. 1989. "Self-Interest and Public Opinion toward Smoking Restrictions and Cigarette Taxes." *Public Opinion Quarterly* 53:1–16.

Green, John C., and James L. Guth. 1991. "Religion, Representatives, and Roll Calls." *Legislative Studies Quarterly* 26:571–84.

Green, John C., James L. Guth, Corwin E. Schmidt, and Lyman A. Kellstedt, eds. 1996. *Religion and the Culture Wars: Dispatches from the Front.* Boulder, CO: Rowman and Littlefield.

Green, John C., Mark J. Rozell, and Clyde Wilcox, eds. 2003. *The Christian Right in American Politics: Marching to the Millennium.* Washington, DC: Georgetown University Press.

Gulati, Girish J. 2004. "Revisiting the Link between Electoral Competition and Policy Extremism in the U.S. Congress." *American Politics Research* 32:495–520.

Haider-Markel, Donald P., Mark R. Joslyn, and Chad J. Kniss. 2000. "Minority Group Interests and Political Representation: Gay Elected Officials in the Policy Process." *Journal of Politics* 62:568–77.

Hall, Richard L. 1996. *Participation in Congress.* New Haven: Yale University Press.

Hall, Richard L., and Alan V. Deardorff. 2006. "Lobbying as Legislative Subsidy." *American Political Science Review* 100:69–84.

Hall, Richard L., and Frank W. Wayman. 1990. "Buying Time: Moneyed Interests and the Mobilization of Bias in Congressional Committees." *American Political Science Review* 84:797–820.

Heckman, James J., and James M. Snyder Jr. 1997. "Linear Probability Models of the Demand for Attributes with an Empirical Application to Estimating the Preferences of Legislators." *RAND Journal of Economics* 28:S142–89.

Herrick, Rebekah, Michael K. Moore, and John R. Hibbing. 1994. "Unfastening the Electoral Connection: The Behavior of U.S. Representatives When Reelection is No Longer a Factor." *Journal of Politics* 56:214–27.

Hibbing, John R. 1991. *Congressional Careers: Contours of Life in the U.S. House of Representatives.* Chapel Hill: University of North Carolina Press.

Hibbing, John R., and Elizabeth Theiss-Morse. 2002. *Stealth Democracy: Americans' Beliefs about How Government Should Work.* New York: Cambridge University Press.

Hill, Kim Quaile, and Angela Hinton-Andersson. 1995. "Pathways of Representation: A Causal Analysis of Public Opinion-Policy Linkages." *American Journal of Political Science* 39:324–35.

Hill, Kim Quaile, and Patricia A. Hurley. 1999. "Dyadic Representation Reappraised." *American Journal of Political Science* 43:109–37.

———. 2002. "Symbolic Speeches in the U.S. Senate and Their Representational Implications." *Journal of Politics* 64:219–31.

Hinich, Melvin J., and Michael C. Munger. 1994. *Ideology and the Theory of Political Choice.* Ann Arbor: University of Michigan Press.

Hochschild, Jennifer L. 2001. "Where You Stand Depends on What You See: Connections among Values, Perceptions of Fact, and Political Prescriptions." In *Citizens and Politics: Perspectives from Political Psychology,* ed. James H. Kuklinski and Dennis Chong. New York: Cambridge University Press.

Huntington, Samuel P. 1950. "A Revised Theory of American Party Politics." *American Political Science Review* 44:669–77.

Hurley, Patricia A. 1982. "Collective Representation Reappraised." *Legislative Studies Quarterly* 7:119–36.

Hurley, Patricia A., and Kim Quaile Hill. 2003. "Beyond the Demand-Input Model: A Theory of Representational Linkages." *Journal of Politics* 65:304–26.

Hutchings, Vincent L. 2003. *Public Opinion and Democracy Accountability: How Citizens Learn about Politics.* Princeton, NJ: Princeton University Press.

Jackson, John E., and David C. King. 1989. "Public Goods, Private Interests, and Representation." *American Political Science Review* 83:1143–64.

Jackson, John E., and John W. Kingdon. 1992. "Ideology, Interest Group Scores, and Legislative Votes." *American Journal of Political Science* 36:805–23.

Jacobs, Lawrence R., and Robert Y. Shapiro. 2000. *Politicians Don't Pander: Political Manipulation and the Loss of Democratic Responsiveness.* Chicago: University of Chicago Press.

Jacobson, Gary C. 2004. *The Politics of Congressional Elections.* 6th ed. New York: Longman.

Jones, Bryan D., Jeffrey Talbert, and Matthew Potoski. 2003. "Uncertainty and Political Debate: How the Dimensionality of Political Issues Gets Reduced in the Legislative Process." In *Uncertainty in American Politics,* ed. Barry C. Burden. New York: Cambridge University Press.

Jones, Charles O. 1961. "Representation in Congress: The Case of the House Agriculture Committee." *American Political Science Review* 55:358–67.

Kalt, Joseph P., and Mark A. Zupan. 1990. "The Apparent Ideological Behavior of Legislators: Testing for Principal-Agent Slack in Political Institutions." *Journal of Law and Economics* 33:103–30.

Kau, James B., and Paul H. Rubin. 1979. "Self-Interest, Ideology, and Logrolling in Congressional Voting." *Journal of Law and Economics* 22:365–84.

Kessler, Daniel, and Keith Krehbiel. 1996. "Dynamics of Cosponsorship." *American Political Science Review* 90:1–12.

King, David C. 1997. "The Polarization of Political Parties and Mistrust of Government." In *Why People Don't Trust Government*, ed. Joseph S. Nye, Philip Zelikow, and David C. King. Cambridge: Harvard University Press.

———. 2003. "Congress, Polarization, and Fidelity to the Median Voter." Unpublished manuscript, Kennedy School of Government, Harvard University.

Kingdon, John W. 1989. *Congressmen's Voting Decisions*. 3rd ed. Ann Arbor: University of Michigan Press.

Koch, Jeffrey W. 2000. "Do Citizens Apply Gender Stereotypes to Infer Candidates' Ideological Orientations?" *Journal of Politics* 62:414–29.

Koger, Gregory. 2003. "Position Taking and Cosponsorship in the U.S. House." *Legislative Studies Quarterly* 28:225–46.

Krajnak, Judith A. 2003. "The Social Construction of Policy: How the Personal and Professional Life Experiences of Female State Lawmakers are Broadening the Debates on Health." Paper presented at the annual meeting of the American Political Science Association.

Krehbiel, Keith. 1991. *Information and Legislative Organization*. Ann Arbor: University of Michigan Press.

———. 1993a. "Constituency Characteristics and Legislative Preferences." *Public Choice* 76:21–37.

———. 1993b. "Where's the Party?" *British Journal of Political Science* 23: 235–66.

———. 1999. "The Party Effect from A to Z and Beyond." *Journal of Politics* 61:832–40.

Lamb, Karl A. 1998. *Reasonable Disagreement: Two U.S. Senators and the Choices They Make*. New York: Garland.

Lane, Robert E. 1962. *Political Ideology*. New York: Free Press.

Lascher, Edward L., Jr., Steven Kelman, and Thomas J. Kane. 1993. "Policy Views, Constituency Pressure, and Congressional Action on Flag Burning." *Public Choice* 76:79–102.

LeoGrande, William M., and Alena S. Jeydel. 1997. "Using Presidential Election Returns to Measure Constituent Ideology." *American Politics Quarterly* 25:3–18.

Levitt, Steven D. 1997. "How Do Senators Vote? Disentangling the Role of Voter Preferences, Party Affiliation, and Senator Ideology." *American Economic Review* 87:425–41.

Lublin, David. 1997. *The Paradox of Representation*. Princeton, NJ: Princeton University Press.

Maltzman, Forrest. 1999. *Competing Principals: Committees, Parties, and the Organization of Congress*. Ann Arbor: University of Michigan Press.

Mansbridge, Jane J. 1999. "Should Blacks Represent Blacks and Women Represent Women? A Contingent 'Yes.'" *Journal of Politics* 61:628–57.

———. 2003. "Rethinking Representation." *American Political Science Review* 97:515–28.

Martin, Paul S. 2003. "Voting's Rewards: Voter Turnout, Attentive Publics, and Congressional Allocation of Federal Money." *American Journal of Political Science* 47:110–27.

Mayhew, David R. 1974. *Congress: The Electoral Connection.* New Haven: Yale University Press.

———. 2000. *America's Congress: Actions in the Public Sphere, James Madison through Newt Gingrich.* New Haven: Yale University Press.

McCarty, Nolan, Keith T. Poole, and Howard Rosenthal. 2001. "The Hunt for Party Discipline in Congress." *American Political Science Review* 95:673–88.

McCrone, Donald J., and James H. Kuklinski. 1979. "The Delegate Theory of Representation." *American Journal of Political Science* 23:278–300.

McDermott, Monika L. 2005. "Candidate Occupations and Voter Information Shortcuts." *Journal of Politics* 67:201–19.

McGuire, Robert A., and Robert L. Ohsfeldt. 1989. "Self-Interest, Agency Theory, and Political Voting Behavior: The Ratification of the United States Constitution." *American Economic Review* 79:219–34.

Miller, Mark C. 1995. *The High Priests of American Politics: The Role of Lawyers in American Political Institutions.* Knoxville: University of Tennessee Press.

Miller, Warren E., and Donald E. Stokes. 1963. "Constituency Influence in Congress." *American Political Science Review* 57:45–56.

Moe, Terry M. 2003. "Reform Blockers." *Education Next* 3:56–61.

Mooney, Christopher Z. 1999. *The Public Clash of Private Values: The Politics of Morality Policy.* Chatham, NJ: Chatham House Press.

Nisbet, Matthew C. 2004. "The Polls-Trends: Public Opinion about Stem Cell Research and Human Cloning." *Public Opinion Quarterly* 68:131–54.

Norris, Pippa, and Ronald Inglehart. 2004. *Sacred and Secular: Religion and Politics Worldwide.* New York: Cambridge University Press.

Oldmixon, Elizabeth A. 2005. *Uncompromising Positions: God, Sex, and the U.S. House of Representatives.* Washington, DC: Georgetown University Press.

Page, Benjamin I., and Robert Y. Shapiro. 1992. *The Rational Public.* Chicago: University of Chicago Press.

Page, Benjamin I., Robert Y. Shapiro, Paul W. Gronke, and Robert M. Rosenberg. 1984. "Constituency, Party, and Representation in Congress." *Public Opinion Quarterly* 48:741–56.

Parker, Glenn R. 1992. *Institutional Change, Discretion, and the Making of the Modern Congress: An Economic Interpretation.* Ann Arbor: University of Michigan Press.

Parker, Glenn R., and Jun Young Choi. 2006. "Barriers to Competition and the Effect of Political Shirking: 1953–1992." *Public Choice* 126:297–315.

Peltzman, Sam. 1984. "Constituent Influence and Congressional Voting." *Journal of Law and Economics* 27:181–210.

Petrocik, John R. 1996. "Issue Ownership in Presidential Elections, with a 1980 Case Study." *American Journal of Political Science* 40:825–50.

Pitkin, Hanna F. 1967. *The Concept of Representation.* Berkeley and Los Angeles: University of California Press.

Poole, Keith T., and Howard Rosenthal. 1997. *Congress: A Political-Economic History of Roll Call Voting.* New York: Oxford University Press.

Popkin, Samuel L. 1994. *The Reasoning Voter.* 2nd ed. Chicago: University of Chicago Press.

———. 2000. *Bowling Alone: The Collapse and Revival of American Community.* New York: Simon and Schuster.

Rohde, David W. 1991. *Parties and Leaders in the Postreform House.* Chicago: University of Chicago Press.

Rokeach, Milton. 1973. *The Nature of Human Values.* New York: Free Press.

Roscoe, Douglas D., and Shannon Jenkins. 2005. "A Meta-Analysis of Campaign Contributions' Impact on Roll Call Voting." *Social Science Quarterly* 86:52–68.

Sanbonmatsu, Kira. 2002a. *Democrats, Republicans, and the Politics of Women's Place.* Ann Arbor: University of Michigan Press.

———. 2002b. "Gender Stereotypes and Vote Choice." *American Journal of Political Science* 46:20–34.

Schiller, Wendy J. 1995. "Senators as Political Entrepreneurs: Using Bill Sponsorship to Shape Legislative Agendas." *American Journal of Political Science* 39:186–203.

———. 2000. *Partners and Rivals: Representation in U.S. Senate Delegations.* Princeton, NJ: Princeton University Press.

Sellers, Patrick J. 1998. "Strategy and Background in Congressional Campaigns." *American Political Science Review* 92:159–71.

Shapiro, Catherine R., David W. Brady, Richard A. Brody, and John A. Ferejohn. 1990. "Linking Constituency Opinion and Senate Voting Scores: A Hybrid Explanation." *Legislative Studies Quarterly* 15:599–621.

Shapiro, Joseph P. 1993. *No Pity: People with Disabilities Forging a New Civil Rights Movement.* New York: Crown.

Sharfstein, Joshua. 1998. "1996 Congressional Campaign Priorities of the AMA: Tackling Tobacco or Limiting Malpractice Awards?" *American Journal of Public Health* 88:1233–36.

Shepsle, Kenneth A., and Barry R. Weingast. 1987. "The Institutional Foundations of Committee Power." *American Political Science Review* 81:85–105.

Sigelman, Lee, and Langche Zeng. 2000. "Analyzing Censored and Sample-Selected Data with Tobit and Heckit Models." *Political Analysis* 8:167–82.

Sinclair, Barbara. 1989. *Transformation of the U.S. Senate.* Baltimore: Johns Hopkins University Press.

Snyder, James M., Jr. 1992. "Artificial Extremism in Interest Group Ratings." *Legislative Studies Quarterly* 17:19–45.

Snyder, James M., and Tim Groseclose. 2000. "Estimating Party Influence in Congressional Roll-Call Voting." *American Journal of Political Science* 44:193–211.

Stonecash, Jeffrey M., Mark D. Brewer, and Mack D. Mariani. 2002. *Diverging Parties: Change, Realignment, and Party Polarization.* Boulder, CO: Westview Press.

Studlar, Donley T. 2002. *Tobacco Control: Comparative Politics in the United States and Canada.* Orchard Park, NY: Broadview Press.

Swain, Carol M. 1993. *Black Faces, Black Interests: The Representation of African Americans in Congress.* Cambridge: Harvard University Press.

Swers, Michele L. 2002. *The Difference Women Make: The Policy Impact of Women in Congress.* Chicago: University of Chicago Press.

Talbert, Jeffrey C., and Matthew Potoski. 2002. "Setting the Legislative Agenda: The Dimensional Structure of Bill Cosponsoring and Floor Voting." *Journal of Politics* 64:864–91.

Tate, Katherine. 2001. "The Political Representation of Blacks in Congress: Does Race Matter?" *Legislative Studies Quarterly* 26:623–38.

Thomas, Sue. 1994. *How Women Legislate.* New York: Oxford University Press.

Tobin, James. 1958. "Estimation of Relationships for Limited Dependent Variables." *Econometrica* 50:24–36.

Uslaner, Eric M. 1999. *The Movers and the Shirkers: Representatives and Ideologues in the Senate.* Ann Arbor: University of Michigan Press.

Van Doren, Peter M. 1990. "Can We Learn the Causes of Congressional Decisions from Roll-Call Data?" *Legislative Studies Quarterly* 15:311–40.

Van Dunk, Emily. 1998. "Handgun Safety and the Making of Controversial Public Policy: An Examination of State Policy Formation." Paper presented at the Annual Meeting of the American Political Science Association, Boston.

Vega, Arturo, and Juanita M. Firestone. 1995. "The Effects of Gender on Congressional Behavior and the Substantive Representation of Women." *Legislative Studies Quarterly* 20:213–22.

Verba, Sidney, Kay Lehman Schlozman, and Henry E. Brady. 1995. *Voice and Equality: Civic Volunteerism in American Politics.* Cambridge: Harvard University Press.

Washington, Ebonya. 2005. "Female Socialization: How Daughters Affect Their Legislator Fathers' Voting on Women's Issues." Unpublished manuscript, Yale University.

Wattenberg, Martin P. 1991. *The Rise of Candidate-Centered Politics: Presidential Election of the 1980s.* Cambridge: Harvard University Press.

Wawro, Gregory. 2001a. *Legislative Entrepreneurship in the U.S. House of Representatives.* Ann Arbor: University of Michigan Press.

———. 2001b. "A Panel Probit Analysis of Campaign Contributions and Roll-Call Votes." *American Journal of Political Science* 45:563–79.

Weissberg, Robert. 1978. "Collective vs. Dyadic Representation in Congress." *American Political Science Review* 72:535–47.

Whitby, Kenny J. 1997. *The Color of Representation: Congressional Behavior and Black Interests.* Ann Arbor: University of Michigan Press.

Wilkerson, John D., and David Carrell. 1999. "Money and Medicine: The American Medical PAC's Strategy of Giving in House Races." *Journal of Health Politics, Policy, and Law* 24:235–55.

Wright, John R. 1998. "Tobacco Industry PACs and the Nation's Health: A Second Opinion." In *The Interest Group Connection: Electioneering, Lobbying, and Policymaking in Washington,* ed. Paul S. Herrnson, Ronald G. Shaiko, and Clyde Wilcox. Chatham, NJ: Chatham House Press.

Wrighton, J. Mark, and Peverill Squire. 1997. "Uncontested Seats and Electoral Competition for the U.S. House of Representatives over Time." *Journal of Politics* 59:452–68.

Zaller, John R. 1992. *The Nature and Origins of Mass Opinion.* New York: Cambridge University Press.

Index